To Kath
with much love for our
long years of "kinship" —
and thanks for your help
in the early stages of this book.

HOME GARDENING HANDBOOKS

GENERAL EDITOR, EDWIN F. STEFFEK
Editor Emeritus, *Horticulture*

Alice Recknagel Ireys, author of *How to Plan and Plant Your Own Property,* is a member of the American Society of Landscape Architects and a registered Landscape Architect in New York State. A graduate of the Cambridge School of Architecture and Landscape Architecture, she is in independent practice in New York. She lectures to garden clubs and design schools and has been an instructor in landscape gardening at Connecticut College for Women, a lecturer at the Brooklyn Botanic Garden, and has contributed to *Horticulture* and *Plants and Gardens* and to the garden pages of the *New York Times.*

ALICE RECKNAGEL IREYS

Small Gardens for City and Country

a guide to designing and planting
your green spaces

A SPECTRUM BOOK

Prentice-Hall, Inc., *Englewood Cliffs, New Jersey 07632*

Library of Congress Cataloging in Publication Data

IREYS, ALICE RECKNAGEL.
    Small gardens for city and country.

    (Home gardening handbooks)   (A Spectrum Book)
    Includes index.
    1. Landscape gardening.   I. Title.   II. Series.
SB473.I73   712'.6   77-5427
ISBN 0-13-813063-9
ISBN 0-13-813055-8 pbk.

PHOTO CREDITS

MOLLY ADAMS: Figures 3–17, 3–31, 3–32, 3–38, 3–45, 3–48; 6–2, 6–3, 6–12, 6–16, 6–39; 7–3, 7–4, 7–9, 7–11, 7–13, 7–14, 7–23, 7–25, 7–30, 7–31, 7–33, 7–34, 7–36, 7–40, 7–41, 7–43, 7–44, 7–45, 7–47, 7–48, 7–50, 7–51; 8–7, 8–12, 8–19, 8–26; 9–1, 9–18, 9–19, 9–20, 9–29, 9–32, 9–35, 9–37; color plates 3, 5, 9, 10, 11, 12, 13, 15, 25.

JO-ANN PRICE BAEHR: Figures 3–19, 3–21, 3–23, 3–25, 3–27, 3–29, 3–33, 3–35, 3–36, 3–40, 3–42; 6–30, 6–31; 7–6, 7–37, 7–49; 8–8; 9–21, 9–27, 9–36, 9–52.

SANDRA RUSSELL CLARK: Figures 6–24, 6–26, 6–28; 7–10, 7–16; 8–20, 8–27; 9–38, 9–39.

DAVID B. EISENDRATH: Figure 7–46.

ALLAN GOLDSTEIN: Figures 7–2, 7–15.

JOHN LYNCH: Figures 6–10; 7–35.

GRETA L. OSBORNE: Color plate 4.

CLIFFORD L. PORTER: Color plate 16.

JOHN RHODEN: Figures 3–12, 3–13; color plate 1.

GEORGE ROOS: Figures 3–15, 3–33, 3–37; 6–5, 6–6, 6–14, 6–18, 6–22, 6–33, 6–35, 6–37; 7–1, 7–5, 7–20, 7–21, 7–22, 7–32, 7–38, 7–39, 7–42, 7–51, 7–52, 7–53; 8–9, 8–10, 8–11, 8–14, 8–21, 8–22; 9–2; color plates 2, 6, 7, 8, 17, 18, 22, 23, 24.

JOSEPH G. STANDART III: Figures 6–8, 6–20; 7–24; 8–18; 9–30, 9–31; color plate 14.

EDWIN F. STEFFEK: Color plate 19.

MAX WILKINSON: Color plates 20, 21.

© 1978 by Prentice-Hall, Inc.
Englewood Cliffs, New Jersey 07632

A SPECTRUM BOOK

10 9 8 7 6 5 4 3 2 1

Printed in the United States of America

Prentice-Hall International, Inc., *London*
Prentice-Hall of Australia Pty. Limited, *Sydney*
Prentice-Hall of Canada, Ltd., *Toronto*
Prentice-Hall of India Private Limited, *New Delhi*
Prentice-Hall of Japan, Inc., *Tokyo*
Prentice-Hall of Southeast Asia Pte. Ltd., *Singapore*
Whitehall Books Limited, *Wellington, New Zealand*

contents

6

Landscape Plans for Country Gardens 63

7

DETAIL PLANNING   **Practical Guides to Garden Details** 107

8

**Water, Features,
Furnishings, and Wildlife**   144

9

My Favorite Plants   161

10

Planting Fundamentals 200

Index 208

preface

The purpose of this book is to give ideas and suggestions for small gardens in city and country. Gardens have different meanings for each of us, but for everyone the completed garden is an experience to enjoy and to share. The way you develop your open area into spaces that make you feel happy and at ease is an art—an art that anyone can master. The more you learn, the more time you take to think about outdoor design, to study these pictures and plans, and to note how basic principles of design have been applied, the more pleasure you will have in creating your very own garden.

Some people may prefer a formal layout with a pattern, clipped hedges, and clean-cut lines; others may love free-flowing curves with unrestricted planting. Whatever you desire, remember that the art of landscape design is kindled by the imagination, providing results that can be uniquely yours.

This book will lead you through the gates of many small gardens tucked away behind old houses in the city as well as into out-of-town gardens scattered throughout the country. Part 1 deals with the planning of city gardens, Part 2 deals with small gardens in the country, and Part 3 contains information on detail planning applicable to both country and city spaces.

acknowledgments

I wish to express my appreciation to all who have helped make this book possible. My children's faith in me was the incentive that made this such a pleasant task.

To clients and friends whose places are illustrated*.

To my good friends, Clara Coffey who has given me continued encouragement, Marguerite Bartz and Nina Beckwith for their dedicated help and interest.

To James S. Kennedy, who has drawn the plans for this publication, and given his advice on many details.

To Edwin F. Steffek, who started me off in the right direction.

To the photographers, particularly Molly Adams, for their help in capturing with cameras the design features essential for illustrations.

* All garden designs in this book are those of the author unless otherwise noted.

Gardens
for Brownstone
and Brick

1 what kind of garden for you?

The trend toward urban restoration began in the 1960s when families who had left the cities for suburbia in the forties and fifties discovered that it was not the Utopia they had expected. Many of them decided that they really belonged in the city near business and entertainment. However, demolition was taking place and huge high-rise apartment houses were springing up where the old row houses once stood. People realized that their architectural heritage was being destroyed, and that perhaps the old buildings were worth saving after all. And so the era of restoration of city homes and gardens was born, involving an abundance of work but producing an even greater satisfaction. This is the era of rebellion against conformity—against city apartments, developments, and suburbia. For many people, renovation of the old houses of a bygone gracious era has been an answer to today's search for individuality and roots.

To dwell in a city and yet be able to withdraw from it at the same time sounds like an impossibility. Yet what better way to achieve this than through the city garden—a green oasis tucked away behind an austere façade. It can give us a place for contemplation and peace amidst the hectic bustle of city life. Perhaps this "secret" garden is one key to man's emotional survival in the city.

Secret gardens, in fact, can be found in all cities throughout the country. I know in particular of many in the New York City area, and in the Beacon Hill section of Boston. Philadelphia and Baltimore also have many old homes and gardens that have been restored to their original charm. Interesting hillside gardens are characteristic of San Francisco. Traveling south, some old courtyards in New Orleans have been remodeled into gardens and many more are waiting to be discovered. Savannah has its secluded side gardens, and Charleston, retaining its old world fascination, has gardens both front and back. The Fan section of Richmond is an old neighborhood that has been restored with dignity to make it an ideal living environment.

Small gardens, even those as tiny as twelve feet wide, can create a breathing space for much enjoyable outdoor living. What a feeling of contentment can come from planting a garden and watching it grow! The delight in seeing it mature is worth all the work involved, particularly if you planned it yourself. After all, is there anyone who is not a lover of nature at heart?

Garden spaces vary in size. The purpose for which you plan to use yours makes a great deal of difference in how the design is to be carried out. A young couple may want space for children to play; an older couple might like a garden filled with unusual plants and incorporating some of the Japanese treasures brought back from their travels; a man who works at home may prefer a pattern garden he can look down on from his window. In each of these gardens there must be harmony between the house and the garden, between the inhabitants' needs and the particular way their garden is designed.

What do you want in your garden? You will not be able to include everything, so it is a matter of deciding your priorities and planning as carefully as you would with any room inside the house. If there are teen-agers, you may need space to cook out; if you are a dog fancier you may want an area for your dog to run. Is your garden to be a place to entertain friends? Are you hoping to grow flowers? Some people feel that total privacy is important; others want to see out and be seen.

No matter what you want, a garden will help to create a healthy environment. The oxygen given off by just two trees, a few flowering shrubs, some grass, and ground covers can help to purify the atmosphere near your home. Trees are also essential to a good total environment. Among other functions, they cool the air underneath their branches, absorb city noises, and as their leaves fall, provide mulch to enrich the soil.

The outdoor living space becomes an extension of the house when designed for relaxing, cooking, entertaining, or for the young to play and have their parties. I recall that at one of my son's birthday parties the boys decided to have a watermelon fight with their dessert—nice and messy, but doing no real harm to the outdoor "room"!

Making a garden is a design process. Scale, proportion, and unity have to be considered in the planning. Bearing in mind these design elements you will be better able to imagine and visualize what can be accomplished. There must be easy access, good enclosure, an adequate garden floor, and a focal point of special interest—perhaps architectural use of different levels, walls, mirrors and color, use of potted plants, nightscaping or lighting to make the garden magical at night and when snow is falling.

Scale.   One of the first things to consider is the relative size of an object as it relates to a human being. One must realize that outside scale is treated quite differently from inside scale because there are no confining walls or ceilings. Scale of outside steps, which have wider treads and lower risers than those in the house, is one of the main things to note. If a space is divided into skillfully arranged and related units it will seem larger. Different levels create an impression of greater space, and it is often desirable to raise the plant beds above and around a small paved section. These can also serve as sitting walls and increase the seating capacity.

Proportion, Balance, and Rhythm.   These must also be considered in your design. Proportion, a principle that is found in all arts, requires a pleasing relationship of one part to every other so that the whole effect is comfortable and harmonious. Along with proper proportion in a garden we should also consider balance, since this helps to give a garden stability. Rhythm, which can be accomplished by the repetition of certain plants, gives a sense of movement in a garden.

Unity and Focal Point.   Whether it consists of the placement of certain plants in a border or the way stepping stones are laid, the final landscape design should be unified. Unity, then, is the ultimate aim, pulling your whole plan together and giving it a sense of completeness. A feature is the culminating point—the necessary accent to your garden. This feature, such as a wall, fountain, pool, bench, or sculpture, will be the focal point of your garden.

And so, as you proceed with planning your garden, you'll find answers to questions like these—among those most often asked of me:

- How do we break up the squareness?
- What do we do with a long narrow lot?
- How can we have complete privacy without a closed-in feeling?
- What about a tiny herb garden?
- What do we do when there is no sun?
- How do we cope with drainage problems?
- How can we hide neighboring back yards when either laws or friendliness forbid a high fence?

- What evergreens will grow in a city yard?
- What ground covers can be used besides ivy?
- Are flowers practical in the city?

The line drawings (Figs. 1–1 through 1–10) show examples of designs you can use. Of course, these can be developed quite differently according to existing conditions and personal taste.

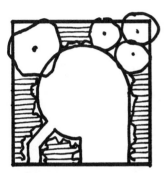

Figs. 1–1, 1–2, and 1–3.   A square lot may be designed with a circle to make it seem larger. A square with the corners cut—French corners—creates a formal arrangement. The third figure shows a garden divided into two separate areas. The size of the garden makes little difference. The important point is to design this open space so that it will be attractive and useful.

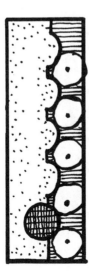

Figs. 1–4 and 1–5.   The long narrow garden can have a very informal plan with a curved walk leading from one terrace to another. Planting each side tends to make it seem longer. Or the plan can be very formal with a definite form repeated often to emphasize the arrangement.

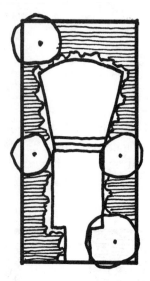

Fig. 1–6. Two separate areas make garden space seem larger. Steps up or down add interest. The secret of success is to divide space so it is an attractive pattern.

Fig. 1–7. Three little connecting circles of different sizes break up this garden yard.

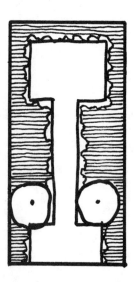

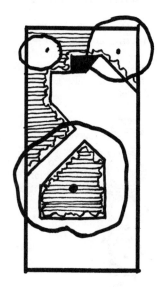

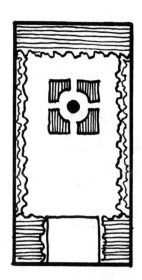

Fig. 1–8. A central path connects two terraces—one near the house and one at back of garden. Flowers and planting each side tend to add length to the arrangement.

Fig. 1–9. This asymmetrical arrangement has divided space into two areas, one near the house and one further away—especially useful if two families are sharing a house and yard.

Fig. 1–10. A pattern garden is pleasant to walk around, but it needs more care than the previous schemes.

2 site conditions

This chapter deals with the existing conditions in your own yard and what can be done with them to create an improved environment not only for your own home but also for the whole community. For example, on one very run-down street in New York, two families bought old houses and carried out renovations by themselves. The work involved in remodeling brought them closer to the different neighborhood ethnic groups and gave them a broader understanding of their community. Beginning with the fixing up of these houses and their front yards, the street was given a complete face lifting and is now the focus of community pride and identification.

"The Street of the Flower Boxes" by Peggy Mann is the true story of a couple who started planting trees and window boxes on one block in an old neighborhood. This sparked the interest of some young people in the

Fig. 2–1.

area who decided to follow the example on another street—a further example of how the physical and aesthetic assets you add around your home can also provide a new vitality to the whole community.

Whether you are renovating an old garden or starting from scratch, the existing site conditions must be carefully examined. Analyze what you have in your outdoor space—trees, poles, sloping ground, drafty corners, little sunshine. Look carefully and note the following items.

Existing Plants. What plants are already present and are they evergreen or deciduous; then decide if you want to keep them. As a rule, old flowering shrubs are not worth saving unless they have a particularly good shape. Evergreens, even if they are slightly scrawny, can be useful as a background—particularly if they are trimmed into an attractive form. Think about the way the Japanese trim their plants in "cloud form." (See Fig. 9–25.) If there are several overgrown privet shrubs you may want to remove the lower branches so that the tops spread to create a shady area.

Overhanging trees, unpruned shrubs, and encroaching vines from adjacent yards often create problems in the city garden. It is legally permissible to cut branches that intrude onto your property, but checking with your neighbor first is the polite thing to do.

If tree work is necessary, it is preferable to have it done before any new planting can be damaged by the falling branches. In some old gardens you may find unusual trees, so don't be too hasty in destroying something that might be considered a landmark.

Exposure. How much light does your garden receive? Will it be a completely shady garden or does one corner have five or six hours of sun? Does the shade come from overhanging branches of existing trees or is it from a twenty-story building? Do any windows of neighboring buildings threaten your privacy? Do you want to close off an ugly view or open up a view of other gardens? The exposure your garden receives will affect the tempera-

Fig. 2–2.

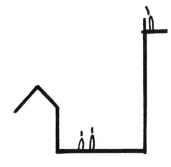

Fig. 2-3.

Fig. 2-4.

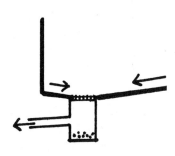

Fig. 2-5.

ture of your planting sites. A southern wall will provide a hardier climate for certain plants. Heating conduits below your garden will also help to maintain a milder temperature.

The number of hours of sunshine and the sunlight location in your yard should be carefully observed. Note particularly if there is a cold air pocket in your yard— i.e., some corner which receives less sun and warmth than the others. Temperature is one of the most important aspects affecting your selection of plants.

Grading and Drainage. Is your garden perfectly flat or does it slope in one or more directions? How much is this pitch? You can figure this quite easily by buying a hand level and checking the difference between the high and the low spots. Incorporating the rise and fall of the garden has to be part of the planning procedure so that steps, walls, or any other structures can be properly constructed.

Backyards that have had no attention given to them may retain undesirable water. In the northeastern United States, for example, we have about forty inches of rainfall a year. It will be necessary to plan for drains to remove surface water promptly so it will not damage the building or form puddles in the yard. Drains should lead to a catch basin which may connect with the drainage system around your house. Perhaps a dry well can be used. This is a deep hole in the ground filled in with rocks, but it can only be used where subsoil is able to absorb water. The paved area leading to the catch basin should slope at the rate of one-fourth inch per foot. A trap at the bottom collects debris and can be easily cleaned every few months. The importance of good drainage and prompt and thorough surface runoff cannot be overemphasized—both for good growing conditions and the avoidance of wet areas in the yard.

Prevailing Air Movements. Both pockets of stagnant air caused by tall buildings and wind gusts between buildings and trees can cause severe harm to certain types of plants. Therefore it is important to select suita-

Fig. 2–6.

ble plant material for the spots subject to such conditions. Certain plants, like dogwood, do not like to be in drafty corners, so take a few minutes on a windy day to observe the air movement in the different parts of your yard. The course of the wind can also affect the removal of impurities, the transmission of sound, and the play of water in a fountain.

It is important to bear in mind that the air of all of our cities is polluted, depending upon the area in which you live. Certain plants, lilacs for example, do not like carbon monoxide and therefore do poorly along a street. Plants able to withstand city conditions are listed in Chapter 9.

Soil. Most existing topsoil in an unused yard needs to have something added to make it capable of engendering proper plant growth. It is usually heavy and lifeless and will need to be worked on. There are two ways to do this. One way is to excavate the old soil, a costly and time-consuming project. I suggest reconditioning the existing soil in your yard, a relatively easy task. First, remove the old debris; then, bring in bales of peat moss to condition the soil. Dig in the peat moss to a depth of two feet. Since peat moss does not have nutrients a fertilizer will also be needed. It is best to do this in the fall and allow it to stand all winter. The soil will then be ready in the spring for additional fertilizing and planting.

The type of fertilizer you use depends on what plants you select. For example, hollies, rhododendrons, and azaleas preferring acid soil need an acid-type fertilizer. The pH value, which is a measure of the acidity or alkalinity of the soil, can be determined by sending a sample to your State Agricultural Experiment Station or by testing it with a simple soil test kit available in most garden stores.

Utilities. There may be overhead wires and poles in your backyard. The chances are that little can be done about their removal. If there are underground pipes or conduits for sewage, electricity, gas, and telephone, it

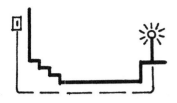

Fig. 2–7.

may be possible to obtain maps from the utility companies to show where these are placed.

If a sprinkler system is to be included so that your plants can be watered automatically, plan for this from the start.

Lighting. Lighting the garden is important not only for security against prowlers, but also for decorative purposes and your own enjoyment after dark. Appropriate placement of outlets allows for permanent safety lights as well as movable fixtures to highlight different plants and features throughout the seasons. Be careful, though—certain plants (such as some of the evergreens) may need special protection if they are close to a bright light.

Plans for outdoor wiring should take into account both the lighting and any electrical pumps needed for waterfalls or fountains. It is a good idea to provide separate switches inside the house for the lights and the pumps, so that the lights may be switched off during the day while the pumps continue to run.

Outdoor wiring must be done by a licensed electrician. Wiring can be temporary or permanent, but most city building codes require permanent installations. Weatherproof outlets should always be used and they can be installed on fence posts, trees, or buildings.

There is much information to obtain as you study the conditions around your home. This knowledge will help you in site planning and designing the open area. In the following chapter you will see plans in which this information and the desires of the owners have been combined in various designs for typical city lots.

3 landscape plans for city gardens

One of the following plans may fit your conditions, but it is more likely that you will pick up and incorporate features from several. No two gardens are ever exactly alike, but there are certain elements each should have such as approach, paving, focal point, and planting.

First, measure your garden carefully (unless you have had a survey) and transfer this information to a piece of graph paper at a scale of one inch equals eight feet. (You can purchase this paper at any art shop.) Now put down the house outline with windows, doors, areaways, and any other existing features. Also note the prevailing site conditions such as trees, any special air movements, and neighboring structures. Be sure to include the north point.

Now sketch out your ideas for locations of paving, steps, walls, and planting beds on tracing paper over the plan you have drawn of your backyard. Then go out in the yard and lay out with red plastic tape or a garden hose the shapes you have planned and take a look from the upstairs window. I have discovered that so many times this will be the most important point from which to observe your garden. Therefore, before you begin the work check this view carefully and decide if your plan will really work.

Whatever plan you develop will be the basis for all future work. Ideas may change as you go along, or you may find some parts of it too costly to build, or it may take longer than you expect. But it is most important to be careful with the initial steps of the plan. Once the construction of the permanent elements is finished, you are ready for the final phase of any landscape work—the planting. Details of planting can be saved until the last, and I have shown planting suggestions in detail in Chapter 9.

Following are plans and pictures of city yards showing what a finished garden can look like. Some of these were designed and built by the owner. I believe they are typical enough of city properties for you to find a number of ideas adaptable to your own yard. The following examples of gardens are represented.

- A studio garden
- A square garden with a pool
- A rectangular garden
- A rectangular garden on two levels
- A city garden with grass
- A sunny garden
- A Victorian garden
- A long narrow garden
- A fan-shaped garden
- A combination garden and parking area
- A Japanese garden
- An oval garden
- A contemporary garden for entertaining
- A place to summer house plants
- A shallow garden for an eighteenth-century house
- A pattern garden
- A garden for a historic house

A STUDIO GARDEN

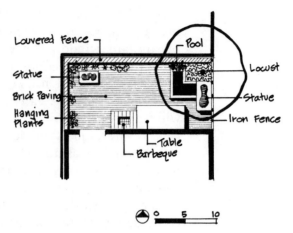

Louvered Fence
Pool
Statue
Locust
Brick Paving
Statue
Hanging Plants
Iron Fence
Table
Barbeque

Fig. 3–1.

0   5   10

This studio of a well-known sculptor was once an old garage, now remodeled into a beautiful home with plenty of space for several big workshops. Behind the large living room there was an areaway eleven by twenty-four feet that was made into a sitting garden with many hanging baskets, potted plants, and bronze figures.

This small space, once filled with rubbish, was cleaned out, brick paving was put down, and raised walls were erected on which a screen of salvaged boards was built. These boards, weathered a lovely soft gray, were taken from an old building being demolished nearby. Boards are placed at a forty-five-degree angle to give protection from the neighbors' windows.

Opposite the door a bronze sculpture of a young girl invites you into the garden room. At the other end of this tiny garden there is a square pool, water tumbling over granite boulders salvaged when telephone cables were being laid in the street. Here a beautiful bronze lion stands guard.

The only permanent planting is one locust tree grown from seed, standing in the corner and cut back each winter to keep it within bounds. Small-scale furniture has been selected to make this a delightful sitting area that is always cool and refreshing.

Designed by JOHN RHODEN.

Fig. 3–2.

Fig. 3–3.

A SQUARE GARDEN

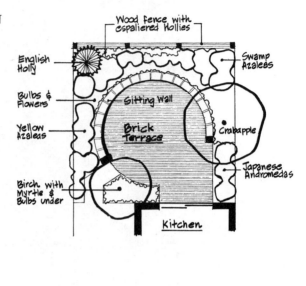

Fig. 3–4.

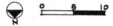

A nineteenth-century brick house with an extension taking up a substantial amount of the rear property left only a small area twenty-five by twenty-five feet for a garden. Opening directly from a remodeled kitchen–family room, a circular design seemed the best solution to soften the squareness of the area and make it seem larger. The brick paving with a low retaining sitting wall provides ample space for outdoor parties. This was one of the requests of the family which includes three young children.

Since this yard receives a great deal of sun, there are plenty of flowers in the raised beds. Directly opposite the door an espaliered Japanese holly grows against the wooden fence. A birch tree softens the corners of the kitchen wing and provides interesting shadows on the wide glass doors. An existing crab apple gives abundant color in May followed by yellow fruit in the fall. Below this crab apple are cotoneasters and dwarf hollies.

All of these plants in the raised beds have been selected for blooming at different times as well as for

Fig. 3–2.

Fig. 3–3.

A SQUARE GARDEN

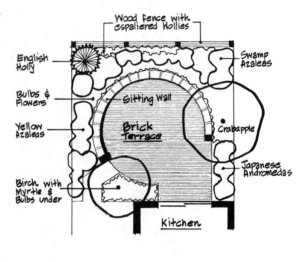

Wood fence with espaliered hollies

English Holly

Swamp Azaleas

Bulbs & Flowers

Sitting Wall

Brick Terrace

Yellow Azaleas

Crabapple

Japanese Andromedas

Birch with Myrtle & Bulbs under

Kitchen

Fig. 3–4.

0   5   10

N

A nineteenth-century brick house with an extension taking up a substantial amount of the rear property left only a small area twenty-five by twenty-five feet for a garden. Opening directly from a remodeled kitchen–family room, a circular design seemed the best solution to soften the squareness of the area and make it seem larger. The brick paving with a low retaining sitting wall provides ample space for outdoor parties. This was one of the requests of the family which includes three young children.

Since this yard receives a great deal of sun, there are plenty of flowers in the raised beds. Directly opposite the door an espaliered Japanese holly grows against the wooden fence. A birch tree softens the corners of the kitchen wing and provides interesting shadows on the wide glass doors. An existing crab apple gives abundant color in May followed by yellow fruit in the fall. Below this crab apple are cotoneasters and dwarf hollies.

All of these plants in the raised beds have been selected for blooming at different times as well as for their interesting shapes in the winter. In the spring the open areas are filled with bulbs but as city bulbs do not have a chance to ripen properly it is much better to remove them when they have finished blooming and then to plant annuals.

Fig. 3–5.

A SQUARE GARDEN
WITH POOL

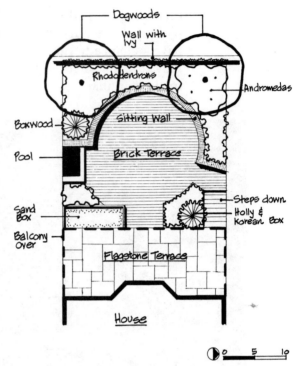

Fig. 3–6.

A very tall town house which commands a fine view of
the New York City skyline from its upper windows has a
garden below the level of the public waterfront espla-
nade. The garden, twenty-five by twenty-five feet, was
designed as a self-sufficient little enclosure for the young
children to play in and for dining on nice evenings. As in
the previous plan, a circle seemed the best way to design
the square area with the added interest of a fountain.

Access from the dining room is by wrought iron
steps to the brick garden with a sitting wall terminated
by the fountain. An awning comes down to protect the
dining area and gives shade at noontime when the children are likely to use it. When the children outgrow the
present play area and sandbox, these spaces can be filled
with flowers.

Dogwoods in the corner and Boule de Neige
rhododendrons with hollies and boxwood complete the

evergreen effect for year-round interest. Pots of geraniums and petunias are put out each year and the fence is covered by an old Peace Rose which blooms all summer.

Fig. 3–7.

A RECTANGULAR GARDEN

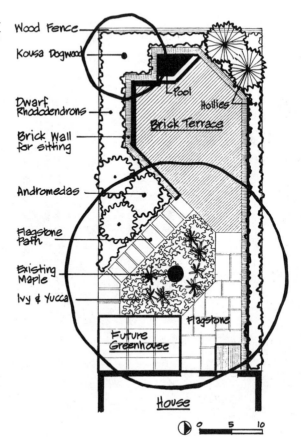

Wood Fence

Kousa Dogwood

Dwarf Rhododendrons

Brick Wall for sitting

Andromedas

Flagstone Path

Existing Maple

Ivy & Yucca

Pool

Hollies

Brick Terrace

Flagstone

Future Greenhouse

House

Fig. 3–8.

0   5   10

A young couple remodeled a four-story house in an old section into a basement and first floor duplex for their use and the two upper floors for renting. The garden, twenty-five by fifty feet, opens directly off the lower living room with a seventy-year-old silver maple giving ample shade to the back of the house. The prime consideration was to provide a place to relax which needed little maintenance. Several plans were presented and the one we see here was finally followed. The owners did most of the work themselves.

A large paved sitting area with a little pool gives them plenty of space for relaxing and entertaining at a distance from the house. In the small paved area adja-

cent to the living room there is space for a table for dining, and eventually part of this area can be developed
into a small working greenhouse.

The raised wall gives ample space for sitting as well
as for displaying the indoor plants. The flagstone path
with its various levels gives a nice circulation pattern
around the existing root structure of the old tree. The
yuccas at the base of the tree were left there to give
stately bloom in the summer time.

Notice particularly the wide board fence placed to
be attractive on both sides and stained a dark brown in
order to play up the hanging baskets and other plants on
the shelf between the boards.

Planting includes Japanese holly, azaleas, and dwarf
rhododendrons. In the corner behind the pool there is a
Chinese dogwood which blooms in June and has delightful strawberry-like fruit lasting a long time into
the fall.

Fig. 3–9.

A RECTANGULAR GARDEN ON TWO LEVELS

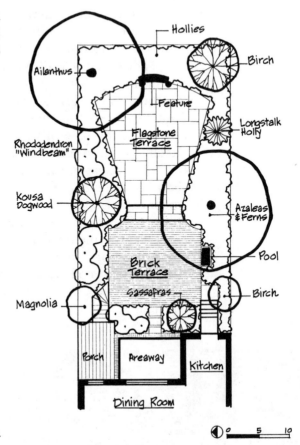

Fig. 3–10.

This typical city backyard only twenty-five by fifty feet gives the feeling of a much larger area. This effect was achieved by a design on two levels and is also helped by trimming the branches of the two existing ailanthus trees very high, producing a cathedral-like atmosphere. The brick terrace close to the house is used for dining and relaxation, and a tiny fountain drips water into an old painted iron sink. The upper area is paved with flagstone in a fan shape, and it is here that the garden feature is located, a group of cherubs playing musical instruments.

Predominantly an evergreen garden, there are a few plants that give color such as the Chinese dogwood, deciduous azaleas, and rhododendron Windbeam. Potted plants are also used—white impatiens around the figures and coleus at the steps. A complete feeling of privacy is achieved so that the space becomes a restful, quiet area. This yard will easily accommodate twenty-five people.

Since ground covers of ivy and ferns are used over most of the planting surfaces, maintenance for such a garden is minimal, requiring only watering in dry seasons, feeding in early April, and trimming in June and September. In addition, it is beneficial to hose the soot off the foliage about once a week.

Fig. 3–11.

**A CITY GARDEN
WITH GRASS**

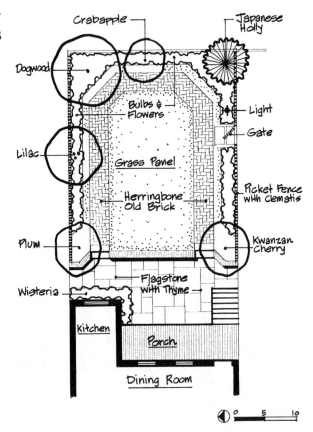

Fig. 3–12.

A city yard twenty-four by forty-four feet with a central lawn gives a lovely feeling of spaciousness. Designed in keeping with the early nineteenth-century façade, the brick paths form a neat walk around the grass panel. The bricks from an old spice warehouse kept their lovely fragrance for a long time after they were laid. The pattern, herringbone, is laid on a bed of concrete with joints of sand in which thyme is growing.

The lower terrace of flagstone has a low brick wall with bluestone coping—ideal for sitting—and is easily accessible to the basement level.

The picket fence, in keeping with the surroundings, is painted a soft cream color which adds light to the garden.

Beds for spring bulbs followed by annuals, impatiens, and begonias and later by chrysanthemums give color until the snow falls. Ferns, mint, funkia, and ivy make a rich green carpet in the remaining areas.

For permanent planting, the remnants of several old Japanese hollies were pruned in an interesting way to give the "cloud effect." A very old lilac still bears blooms. The new planting included a Kwanzan cherry, a plum, and a dogwood.

An automatic sprinkler system was installed when the garden was designed so that the grass could be watered throughout the summer when the family is away.

A narrow wooden porch in keeping with the architecture of the house looks down on the garden and serves as a pleasant place for a cup of tea.

Designed by owner.

Fig. 3–13.

A SUNNY GARDEN

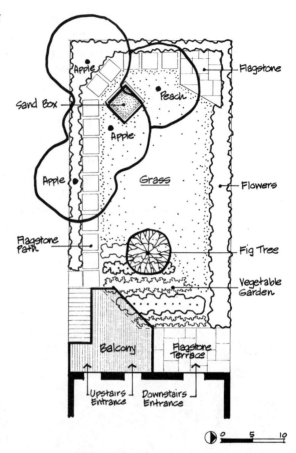

Fig. 3–14.

A garden twenty-five by fifty feet in the center of several open yards has been divided into an interesting pattern for two families. The triangular deck serves the owners who live on the upper two floors. The family in the basement apartment can use the small terrace beneath the deck, surrounded by a vegetable and herb garden shared by both families.

The lawn area with its fruit trees produces at least two bushels of apples and one of peaches. Beneath the peach tree is a very tiny terrace just for two, raised above the lawn. From here it is pleasant to look back at the house and watch the young children playing in the sandbox. Remember that grass with dogs and children playing on it has to be fed three times a year and repaired each spring.

Notice the fence—a "grape stake fence" which provides for air to move through the yards but gives some protection. It was made by the owners out of two-by-four-inch boards stretched horizontally to posts six feet on center. Vines grow well on this—even a pyracantha produces an abundance of berries.

The borders are filled with flowers whose continuous bloom makes this city garden as colorful as any in the country. With its informal homey flavor it is both functional and aesthetically pleasing.

Designed by owner.

Fig. 3–15.

**A VICTORIAN
GARDEN**

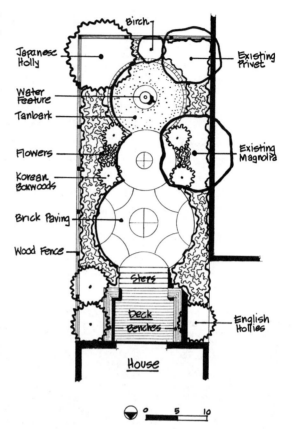

Japanese
Holly

Water
Feature

Tanbark

Flowers

Korean
Boxwoods

Brick Paving

Wood Fence

Birch

Existing
Privet

Existing
Magnolia

Steps

Deck
Benches

English
Hollies

House

Fig. 3–16.

0   5   10

In the rear of a remodeled house in the heart of New York City, a twenty-by-forty-foot garden was designed in the Victorian style to be the focal attraction from the first floor flower room. This room with white wicker furniture and gay plants looks out on the garden with its three small circles and a three-tiered fountain.

The existing conditions included one magnolia tree and several large privets at the rear of the garden. A neighbor's brick wall flanks one side to give privacy; on the remaining two sides a new wooden fence was designed.

The garden slopes to the lowest circle to give greater perspective. Brick paving set in cement provides an easy slope to the fountain circle which is tanbark, practical because it absorbs water, gives a dark color, and makes a soft place to walk.

Lighting enhances the little garden, spotlighting both the fountain and magnolia tree. The low fixtures frame the deck and steps, completing the evening lighting scene.

The small deck with low benches provides a sitting area, but the garden is planned primarily to be looked at during all times of the year. Therefore, it was planted with hollies, small leaf rhododendrons, leucothoe, and Korean boxwood for winter effect. White and yellow azaleas along with many bulbs give color from April to June, and coral impatiens with some caladium plants provide color until frost. The garden, designed also for low maintenance, can easily be taken care of with a few hours' work a week.

Fig. 3–17.

A LONG NARROW GARDEN

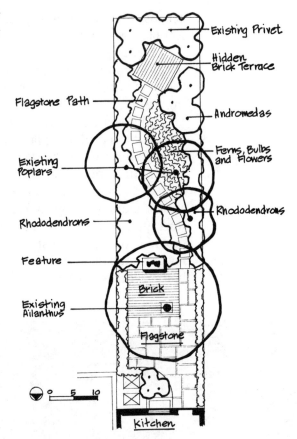

Existing Privet

Hidden Brick Terrace

Andromedas

Flagstone Path

Ferns, Bulbs and Flowers

Existing Poplars

Rhododendrons

Rhododendrons

Feature

Brick

Existing Ailanthus

Flagstone

0   5   10

Fig. 3–18.

Kitchen

A long narrow garden, fourteen by eighty feet, had a very old straight poplar tree directly in the middle of the area and an ailanthus tree near the house. This garden, open and spacious since all fences are chain link, was designed with two small terraces—one near the house and one hidden at the back beneath some very old privet. A flagstone walk joins the two terraces in a pleasant curve.

Beneath the ailanthus tree by the house, the brick paving laid dry in a basket weave pattern has as its focal point an old Indian goddess found at a house wrecking lot. Surrounded by ferns and boxwood, she sits serenely looking down on this restful terrace.

Along the long walk there are flowers in profusion.

Since the area receives a great deal of sunshine, the owners have also planted tomato and pepper plants along with parsley and dill.

Remodeling the house, in an old section of the city, has not only given its owners the garden plus spacious rooms and good architectural detail unavailable in most new houses, but has also stimulated others in the neighborhood to make similar improvements—a good sign of our times.

Fig. 3–19.

A FAN-SHAPED GARDEN

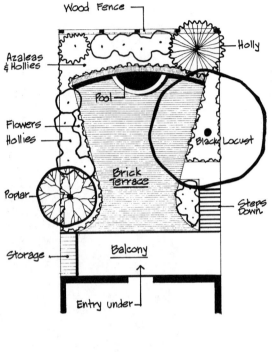

Wood Fence

Holly

Azaleas & Hollies

Pool

Flowers

Hollies

Black Locust

Poplar

Brick Terrace

Steps Down

Balcony

Storage

Entry under

Fig. 3–20.

Over the years this garden design has been changed several times. The one you see here is planned for outdoor dining and as a play area for the grandchildren. The stately locust, now sixty feet tall, was originally brought in as a little seedling in the owner's pocket. Over the years it has grown and flourished and its lacy branches cool the upstairs rooms.

The design in the shape of a fan has wide borders filled with evergreens and flowers so that the garden, which is twenty-five by forty feet, is pleasant all year. French doors open directly from the dining room to a small covered area with an awning to give summer shade. Opposite this door, a brick pool with low sitting wall provides the chief attraction for the grandchildren. Cooling sounds from the fountain, as always, add much pleasure to the garden. Directly over the covered area is a small balcony opening from the living room with wrought iron steps leading to the garden.

Planting includes low hollies, azaleas, and rhododendrons. Spring bulbs give color over a two-month period, followed by such standbys as impatiens, begonias, and geraniums.

Fig. 3-21.

**A COMBINATION
GARDEN AND
PARKING AREA**

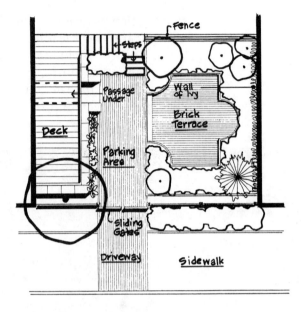

Fig. 3–22.

Designed particularly to solve a parking problem, this garden also provides a space for entertaining.

The lovely nineteenth-century house on a corner plot had space for a garden twenty-five by thirty feet in the rear. When it became necessary to build a new fence, it was decided to make space for parking within the garden, and so it was necessary to drop the curb at the sidewalk. Sliding doors of redwood were constructed wide enough to accommodate the car. The driveway was paved with hard-baked bricks set on edge.

A three-foot-wide stairway leads from the deck down to this brick paving. Ivy covers the wall of the adjacent building, and the beds are filled with evergreens and ground cover. A poplar tree with its narrow upright shape grows near the corner of the upper deck and provides some privacy from the street, and there is even a small terrace underneath the deck.

The slate table is unusual in that it was salvaged

from an old chemical laboratory. It is set on a tile base previously used by the telephone company for coiling cables.

Designed by EDWARDS F. RULLMAN, *Architect.*

Fig. 3–23.

**A JAPANESE
GARDEN**

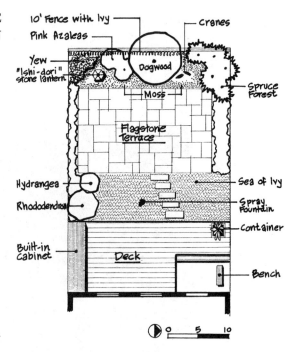

10' Fence with Ivy
Pink Azaleas
Cranes
Yew
"Ishi-dori" stone lantern
Dogwood
Spruce Forest
Moss
Flagstone Terrace
Hydrangea
Sea of Ivy
Rhododendron
Spray Fountain
Container
Built-in Cabinet
Deck
Bench

Fig. 3–24.

0   5   10

This enclosed Japanese garden, twenty-five by twenty-six feet, designed as a foreground to the stunning New York City skyline beyond, is a quiet and contemplative area in which to relax. Looking down from the porch across the sea of ivy and paving, one is very conscious of the "borrowed scenery" constantly changing in color and mood.

It was very fitting to make the garden Japanese for its owners had traveled extensively in the Orient. The wide, open terrace without railing extends over the ivy through which five stepping stones lead down to the lower area.

A carp spouts water which gives a misty, tranquil atmosphere. The *Ishi dori* (stone lantern) was carefully brought back on one of the trips, as well as the beautiful cranes standing guard in their bed of moss.

Planting includes a dogwood pruned round in the center of the planting strip, one upright yew near the lantern, and a few pink azaleas at one corner balanced by a little forest of spruce in the opposite corner. A typical Japanese false perspective was created by planting the

larger leaf rhododendron and hydrangea in the foreground, and the smaller leaf and needle plants at a distance.

The porch of wide redwood boards has a built-in
cabinet with marble top at one end, below which electric
outlets provide plenty of cooking facilites.

Designed by owner.

Fig. 3–25.

Fig. 3–26.

AN OVAL GARDEN

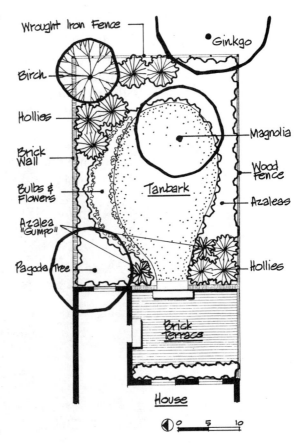

Wrought Iron Fence

Ginkgo

Birch

Hollies

Brick Wall

Bulbs & Flowers

Azalea "Gumpo"

Pagoda Tree

Magnolia

Wood Fence

Azaleas

Tanbark

Hollies

Brick Terrace

House

Fig. 3-27.

0   5   10

In this oval garden, twenty by forty feet, there was an existing magnolia tree in the middle of the lawn area. Over the years, with the changes in the surrounding buildings, it became more difficult to maintain a good lawn owing to the increasing shade. It was then decided to replace the lawn with soft yellow gravel which requires little maintenance and is pleasant to look at all year.

A brick terrace just outside the house has a low wall around it, which is ideal for sitting and for potted plants. Two steps lead up to the garden where the topsoil was removed from the center and a layer of heavy polyethylene was put down. Three inches of run-of-the-bank gravel was then added on top. Holes were perforated around the magnolia in the polyethylene to allow for water and drainage. The brick edging outlines the area and holds the gravel in place.

In the beds there are three varieties of hollies—English, Japanese, and Hellers—and three varieties of azaleas—Delaware Valley White, Narcissiflora, and Gumpo to give spring interest. Bulbs are used in various planting pockets and these little areas are later filled with chrysanthemums for fall color.

Though this little garden is in the heart of a city, within a stone's throw of a river and busy highway, it is completely enclosed, peaceful and quiet.

Fig. 3–28.

A CONTEMPORARY GARDEN FOR ENTERTAINING

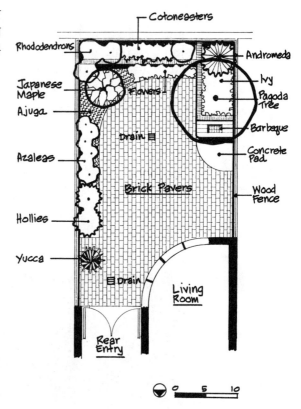

Fig. 3–29.

Remodeled to accommodate a young family with four children, this inner city yard, twenty-five by thirty feet, was designed with ample open area and a built-in gas barbecue. The design, materials, and form reflect the contemporary style of the remodeled town house. A large circular glass window looks out on the garden to give the indoor-outdoor association that is so important. The brick pavers laid in cement with good drainage provide ample space for entertaining. With the seven-foot fence there is a feeling of complete privacy and enclosure while maintaining a clean, uncrowded space.

Wide beds follow the curve of the yard with two levels of planting which help to create a feeling of greater space. Here a Japanese pagoda tree with its arching branches will bloom in August, and the Japanese maple and azaleas give further color accents. Flower borders with spring bulbs are followed by annuals—marigolds and petunias—to provide color throughout the summer. Chrysanthemum plants brought in during the fall continue the flower effect until late autumn.

Designed by JAMES S. KENNEDY, *L.A.*

Fig. 3–30.

**A PLACE
TO SUMMER
HOUSE PLANTS**

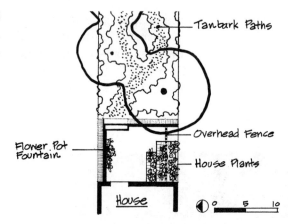

Fig. 3–31.

Just outside a brownstone basement dining room only twelve feet wide, there is a small sunken area barely six feet wide beyond which a fifty-foot-long narrow garden is given over to birds and squirrels. In this small lower area the owners have designed two unusual features. On one of the walls there is a place to summer the house plants. On the other side, there is an amusing little fountain made out of flower pots.

For the construction of the shelves for house plants an existing wall was covered with fencing material and an eight-inch overhang was provided for lighting purposes. Here a sixty-watt fluorescent fixture was set into water-protected sockets for continuous lighting day and night since this area receives very little sunlight. The hanging baskets and other house plants have grown exceedingly well under such unusual conditions.

On an existing ledge against a wooden fence on the opposite side, the owners built a brick back wall for a tiny fountain of flower pots. Water spouts below an old decorative door knocker from a brass fixture and trickles through carefully layered pierced flower pots. The bottom copper tray holds the recirculating pump, well hidden by plants.

The brick, picked up at a nearby demolition site, was laid dry against the fence. Terracotta pots easily available from any garden supplier make the cost of such a project very low. It makes a charming place to hang baskets of spider plants, begonias, and tradescantias.

Designed by owner.

Fig. 3–32.

Fig. 3–33.

**A SHALLOW
GARDEN FOR AN
EIGHTEENTH-
CENTURY HOUSE**

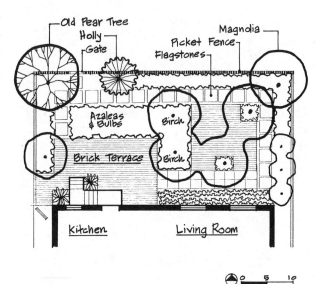

Fig. 3–34.

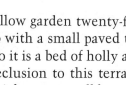

For a historic house a wide, shallow garden twenty-five by fifty feet has been broken up with a small paved terrace near the back stairs. Next to it is a bed of holly and azaleas. Two birch trees give seclusion to this terrace, and the remaining open area which was a small lawn, is now paved with brick. A flagstone path leads around this terrace with a gate in one corner to the next yard. Iron urns painted white and filled with geraniums are placed on the terrace for summer and fall effect. Against the picket fence Japanese holly and Rose of Sharon are growing luxuriantly to provide privacy. Rose of Sharon is one of the large shrubs which grows well in the city with pink, blue, or white flowers, single or double, surviving and blooming for many years.

There is an old pear tree in one corner, a relic of bygone days, which is covered with white blossoms in early May. A bird house hidden in its branches is a miniature replica of the eighteenth-century house itself.

Fig. 3–35.

A PATTERN GARDEN

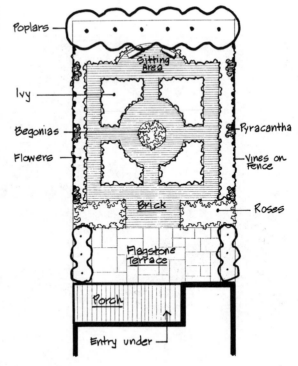

Fig. 3–36.

Looking down on this twenty-five-by-fifty-foot garden at all seasons is a delight and walking around the beds makes one think of the Williamsburg Gardens that have been enjoyed by so many throughout the years.

The four little beds within the square brick paving are filled with Baltic ivy. This is a smaller and slower growing ivy that stays a good rich green.

Rose bushes are close to the flagstone terrace and flowers are planted along the side beds with pyracantha espaliered against the fence. Begonias fill the round bed.

Poplar trees form a background at the rear to hide an apartment building.

Designed by owner.

Fig. 3–37.

**A GARDEN FOR
A HISTORIC HOUSE**

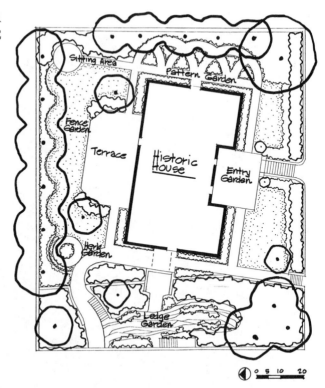

Fig. 3–38.

The Abigail Adams Smith Museum is one of only seven eighteenth-century buildings left in Manhattan. It is maintained by the Colonial Dames of America.

The grounds have been designed and planted in the eighteenth-century style, following the Northern European and particularly Dutch pattern garden influence felt strongly by the early settlers of New York.

A large brick terrace with wooden benches, adjacent to the museum, is often used for receptions. It looks out on the long narrow garden to a little sitting area on the east and a circular herb garden on the west.

The property is enclosed with a colonial board fence covered with English ivy trained in a pattern. A pleached row of Oriental plane trees hides the tall buildings to the north. Below these are beds of ivy and tulips.

The pattern flower garden echoes early American

style; in spring, squills, crocus, and grape hyacinth bloom in the smaller beds; cottage tulips in the larger. Hawthorn trees and old-fashioned summer flowers give continuing color contrast.

The woody material, shrubs, and trees reflect early interest in native American plants, using shadblow and laurel, boxwood, hawthorn and crab apple. Beneath mock orange, viburnum, and flowering quince at the west end are springtime colonies of snowdrops, violets, hosta, wood hyacinth, candytuft, primula, squills, and daffodils.

Fig. 3–39.

Gardens
in the Country

4 planning a country garden

Gardens in the country may bring to your mind vast estates with large flower gardens, ponds, and wide lawns. But what I would like to discuss instead is the small country garden similar to its city cousin. Many of these will be small enough to be both planned and planted by you. Outside the urban areas you have more freedom to choose where to put your garden, and you are usually less restricted in the size of the area and in the selection of plants.

Country gardens can be planted beside a terrace, along a walk, or even at your front door. If a country cottage is near the sea or ski slopes, plant selection will be limited in some respects, but for the most part your plan will still depend on what kind of a dream garden you wish to create. Will it be a year-round garden of evergreens, an herb garden, a plot for summer flowers, or a special addition to your terrace? Will you entertain large groups or is it to be a secluded refuge for two? Is your site in the woods or on the dunes so that you need to design plantings for this type of condition?

The varieties are as endless as your imagination and your interests. If you have traveled to Japan recently you may have come back with a lantern and dipping well and you will want to design a garden in typical Japanese fashion to include these treasures.

Pattern gardens are fun to walk through and are particularly adapted to eighteenth-century houses. The gardens of Williamsburg are elegant examples of traditional pattern gardens set gracefully beside stately homes.

Perhaps your love is house plants and you need a place to summer them. A terrace garden can easily include shelves in a protected corner and hooks for hanging baskets. There can also be space provided so that large plants may be rolled out and positioned in attractive groupings. Be sure to include a dipping well so that you can wash the plants before you bring them in for the winter.

Is your garden to be in a woodland setting or next to your terrace or under one magnificent large maple? In any case, it should be a self-contained unit, but one which also relates well with its surroundings. A little garden sitting by itself in the midst of a large lawn can look very lonesome.

Once you have decided on the purpose of your garden, exactly where you place it will depend largely on the land around your home. When the purpose and location of the garden have been determined you will then have to plan for its size. Family needs, the dimensions of the house, and the existing landscape will be important factors in your plan. For example, if you are wondering how big to make a garden that will be adjacent to your terrace, think of exactly what it will be used for and of how it will look in relation to the terrace itself and to the house. In general, it is better to have it a bit too large than too small—a tiny place can sometimes serve no purpose whatsoever.

To insure that your garden will be attractive, there are certain design principles you have to consider. Perhaps these will be hard to comprehend at first, but you will become more discerning with practice.

Scale.   Scale is the relative size of an object as it relates to a human being. Good appreciation of scale can be achieved by carefully considering the parts of a garden—is the path wide enough to walk two-abreast? Is the access opening wide enough to offer a real welcome? Is the sitting wall a comfortable height?

Proportion.   Proportion is the pleasing and proper relationship of one part to the whole. To achieve good proportion you must again study each part so that the complete garden is at ease with all of its parts.

Unity.   Unity in a composition is achieved with forms and plants of related color and texture. Don't plan a garden or a boundary with such a hodgepodge that the eye is impelled to move restlessly from one plant to another.

Balance.   Symmetrical or asymmetrical, is necessary for a sense of stability. Trees and shrubs evenly arranged around a central feature, such as a grass panel will be in symmetrical balance. A garden door that is not centered needs asymmetrical treatment, such as a shadbush on one side with three low-growing yews on the other.

Rhythm.   Rhythm in design is gained by repeating the same plant or group of plants at regular intervals in order to give a sense of movement. You might also select plants that have the same qualities—such as the different hollies—and then repeat them in rhythmical groupings with other plants. Avoid using a great variety of plants.

Accent.   The climax of your design should draw attention to the focal point which may require plants of special interest. Here is where your unusual and perhaps expensive specimens count the most.

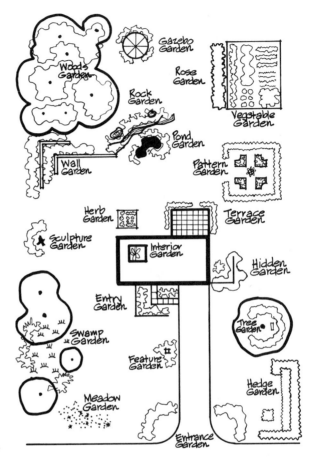

Fig. 4–1.

The sketches show various garden types and shapes (Fig. 4–1). It cannot be over emphasized that a garden should be a self-contained unit using the principles of scale, balance, proportion, unity, rhythm, and accent. Also, because the passage from indoors to outdoors is another important factor in design, plan for easy access to your new garden. Keep in mind all the principles of good design but plan first for the garden's use—as an entertainment area, as a cutting garden, or as whatever your fancy dictates. If it is properly designed and carried out, it will be a beautiful addition to your home and to your life.

5 site conditions

After you determine the location and size of your garden, you will have to analyze the site itself carefully in order to develop a logical plan. Start by sitting in the area at various times of day to get the feel of the surroundings. Notice first how you would enter—by steps? a winding path? all on a level? Are there views or a closed-in feeling? Are there any existing features such as rocks to be considered?

Any site is composed of factors below, above, and on the ground, and it is important to investigate them all in order to plan, construct, and plant your garden. The points discussed below are the most important ones in the analysis of your chosen site.

Below Ground. Do you have a rocky condition? If so, you may have trouble in working out your design.

Fig. 5-1.

Because underground ledges are expensive to blast it is often better to adapt your plan to incorporate them. For example, you can strip the soil to reveal interesting rock pockets, or use outcroppings as important features of your garden.

Is the area newly filled? If so watch for later earth settling. Is there an underground stream? In that case, one spot may stay wet for long periods after a rain and in the spring. In many situations the underground conditions can have a great effect on plants, paving, and maintenance. What about the water table? If it is high, you will need an underground tile system to carry water away. Dig a hole to find out and notice how long the water remains.

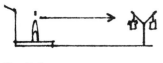

Fig. 5-2.

Above Ground. Are there overhanging branches, telegraph lines, or a neighbor's clothesline that will intrude on your garden view? Such unwanted objects must be noticed early if they are to be effectively hidden or disguised in the final plan.

On the Ground. Is the area level or are there slopes that will need planting and terracing? What sightlines such as clumps of trees, meadows, old or new buildings will you need to open up or shut out? Many subdivisions and shopping areas are changing the face of the countryside so it may be necessary to give up the wide-open feeling and adapt to a smaller concept of an enclosed garden. Some sites have large existing rock ledges and interesting formations. These can be cleared and used effectively as a ledge or rock garden. In one case, we stripped a very large area and put well-rotted manure on it for the winter. In the spring when it was cleared the rock formation had taken on a lovely soft color.

Fig. 5-3.

Exposure. Notice the amount of wind and sun your garden will have in the various months when you will be using it. If it is a very windy area you will need a windbreak like a fence or wall. Some flowers, such as daffodils, always turn their faces toward the sun. If you want to get this sort of special effect careful observation of light conditions is required. A garden developed on the north side is always slower to warm up in the spring but cooler during the hot months.

Grades and Drainage. What are the existing grades and how will they affect the design? A steep, sloping area will need retaining walls and steps, while a very flat area will need some slight pitch to prevent water from pocketing in unattractive spots. Water should drain away from the building, so be sure that paved areas slope properly to a catch basin. Also, water from a downspout has to go somewhere. Is it taken to a storm sewer or a dry well?

Utilities. You should know the location and depth of pipes for your water, sewer, and drain lines as well as the position of telephone and light cables. You should certainly provide outlets for water (perhaps more than one if you are planning to include a fountain feature), one or two electrical outlets, and perhaps even a telephone connection. If you want to have a sprinkler system, include it in the early stages of your plan.

Soil. How much topsoil do you have? Do you need to bring in new soil? Is there a hardpan below that will need to be broken up? Check the depth of your topsoil by digging a hole and noticing how far down this good soil goes. If it goes down only a few inches you will have to do more preparation by digging down at least eighteen inches and adding peat moss or humus. If there is hardpan below your garden you may need to remove this and provide some drainage material as most plants do not like wet feet.

Existing Planting. Are there any trees or shrubs that you wish to keep? Are there any neighbor's trees that might affect your planting?

Maintenance. How much time do you wish to give to this new garden? Are you going to take care of it yourself or have someone to help? Lawns require consid-

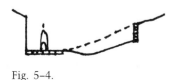

Fig. 5-4.

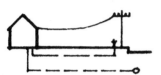

Fig. 5-5.

erably more maintenance than paved space. Different types of gardens vary in their maintenance needs: a flower garden is certainly more time-consuming than an evergreen garden.

Lighting.   Where will you need to install lights for safety so that it is easy to get in and out of your garden in the evening? Do you want to light special areas? You may need a free-standing outlet into which you can put your fixture. If you are wiring for a fountain with switch control, be sure to comply with local codes and ordinances.

It may not seem important at first, and it may be initially difficult to look closely at a particular site with these factors in mind, but a good plan depends a great deal on really seeing what is there and imagining its possibilities.

This initial analysis should be done before you get out the graph paper and work out a design for your new garden. Anyone can design a garden if they are willing to take time to recognize the existing site conditions and apply the principles of design to work out a plan that best suits their needs.

Fig. 5-6.

6 landscape plans for country gardens

A trained eye can tell instantly if the principles of landscape design have been followed in planning a particular garden. I can recall one garden on which I was asked to consult. The instant I entered it I knew that thoughtful study had been given to each part. I mentioned this and the client said, "Yes, thirty years ago, and we have enjoyed it every day since then." All that was needed now was some simple replacement of plant material.

Scale Measurements

If you are starting a garden, the first step is to measure your area carefully. Be sure to get the exact dimensions of the space; then put this information on a piece of graph paper, using one inch equals eight feet or one inch equals ten feet. Either of these scales can be used for this general plan and for the detailed planting plan. Perhaps you have a plot plan which indicates the exact position of the house on the grounds. It does not, however, tell you anything about the grades and it is often necessary to have a topographical survey made of the area where you propose to have your garden. A surveyor will do this for you and his plan will be the basis for you to work out construction details showing where walls, steps, and terraces might be located. If you are doing your own survey be sure to show the north point, existing features such as trees, rock outcrop, and all utilities. Grade differences may be measured by using a line level available at most hardware stores. By careful figuring you will arrive at the information for the different elevations in your garden so that you can plan your construction details.

Terrace Gardens

Let's start with a terrace, since it is one of the easiest kinds of a garden to design and build. Indeed, around almost any paved area there is a wonderful chance to create a garden. You will see how in one terrace garden there is a low brick wall with a planting area for flowers. In another, there is a brick paving with evergreen plants surrounding it for winter interest. And in yet another, there is a wooden deck with flagstone paving below connected with a series of waterfalls. In one of my favorite terrace gardens the area is divided into two separate garden rooms, one for dining and one for relaxing. The upper garden is filled with bulbs and annuals, while the lower has a sitting wall with a perennial border along one side and evergreens along the other.

The Plans

The eighteen plans that follow have been carried out in different regions with varying terrain and conditions. They offer many ideas for the development of your own garden wherever it may be. The following types of country gardens are represented.

- A garden with waterfalls
- Adjoining garden terraces
- A garden terrace with a view
- A shady hillside garden
- A long narrow garden
- A side garden
- An evergreen garden
- A dry stream on a hillside
- A hillside flower garden
- A flower pattern garden
- An herb garden
- Two deck gardens
- An entrance garden
- An overgrown garden revamped
- A tree garden
- A rocky ledge garden
- An early spring garden
- A cottage garden

**A GARDEN
WITH WATERFALLS**

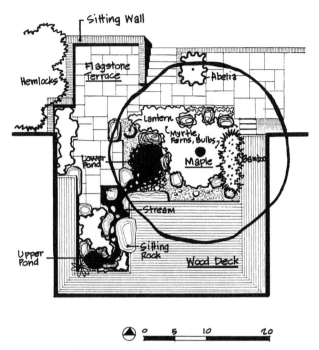

Fig. 6–1.

In an area twenty-four by thirty-two feet between the wings of a house, the owners wanted a new terrace that would include something unusual under the branches of an old Norway maple. They wanted it to look Japanese as a setting for a recently acquired handsome stone lantern. Since this area was very visible from all parts of the house, it was necessary to create a plan that would be exciting throughout the year. Here a small deck and terrace on the lower level were connected by large boulders. Water gushes out beneath a rock in this upper corner and flows in a series of five waterfalls into the basin at the bottom. The deck makes a cozy dining spot close to the kitchen and for larger parties the flagstone terrace below provides ample space. There are several ways to move around both by steps and using the rocks as stepping stones.

Plantings of evergreens, leucothoe, hollies, cotoneasters, and ground covers of epimedium, liriope, myrtle, and ajuga cover the open areas between the rocks.

Even the bamboo used to shield the bedroom windows was selected to give the Japanese effect.

The waterfalls, twisting and turning in this small area, were constructed using native stones from an old quarry. These stones were carefully placed to provide the waterfalls and spillway. A base of four inches of concrete with steel mesh was laid down, on top of which the large boulders were placed. Silicone waterproofing was used throughout and washed gravel four inches deep was placed on top. The submersible pump, Little Giant #3E–12N, placed in the lowest pool is connected by a supply line well hidden to come out at the top and recirculate the water.

Fig. 6–2.

**ADJOINING
GARDEN TERRACES**

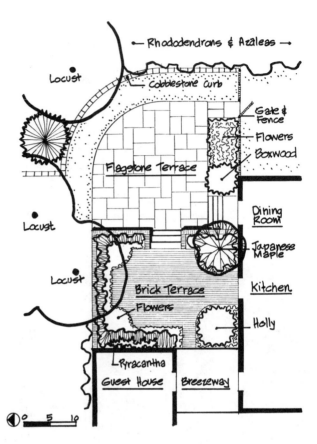

Fig. 6–3.

When a retired couple remodeled a saltbox house, they wanted a small terrace for breakfast and a larger one for entertaining fitted into the available twenty-eight-by-forty-six-foot space. The small upper terrace outside the kitchen is designed to be gay with bulbs in the spring followed by annuals in the summer.

The lower garden, down three steps, has a sitting wall on one side and a perennial border with many summer-blooming flowers. Evergreens, rhododendrons, and hollies follow the curve of the terrace and give a feeling of enclosure. The old locust trees provide shade for this terrace which is easily accessible from the upper garden and the dining room.

It is interesting to note that the flagstone had been brought from the family's previous home and relaid with

Fig. 6–4.

close joints. This can be done very easily provided the flagstone is in good condition. It was two inches thick and laid on a bed of crushed stone with a cushion of sand providing the necessary drainage.

Both terraces overlook the pool which is several feet below and some fifteen feet away, but it is the two terraces themselves which make the outdoor living areas so important and attractive for the warm months of the year.

Fig. 6–5.

**A GARDEN TERRACE
WITH A VIEW**

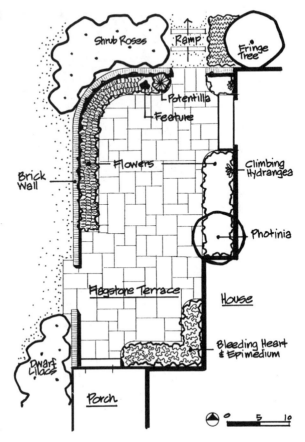

Fig. 6–6.

A sloping area looking towards the Berkshires was a perfect location for a terrace garden. Opening out of three rooms—a library, an enclosed porch, and the master bedroom—it made an outdoor garden room that changed the aspect of both house and site.

This flagstone terrace, twenty by thirty-six feet, with a low wall surrounding it, is used as a sitting area as well as a backdrop for a three-foot bed which is filled with changing blooms. In one corner a statue of St. Francis (the patron saint of nature) seems to speak to the birds and flowers of this quiet little garden.

In the spring 200 bulbs give glorious color during April and May, along with the early perennials, wild blue phlox, Jacob's ladder, and candytuft. Later the peonies, columbine, and iris continue the color until the summer annuals flower in mid-June.

The corner by the library and porch receives very little sun so it is necessary to use shade-loving plants—climbing hydrangea, violets, epimedium, and funkia.

Overlooking the sweep of meadow to the farm pond below, the terrace adds a new dimension to this country home.

Fig. 6–7.

A SHADY HILLSIDE GARDEN

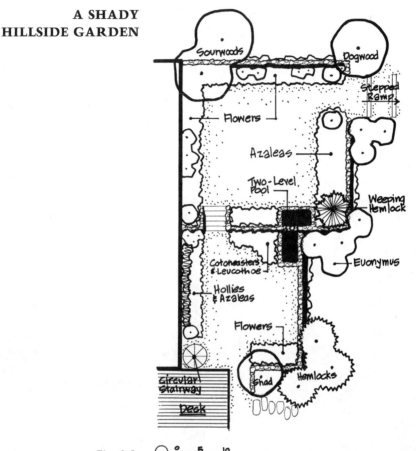

Sourwoods

Dogwood

Stepped Ramp

Flowers

Azaleas

Two-Level Pool

Weeping Hemlock

Euonymus

Cotoneasters & Leucothoe

Hollies & Azaleas

Flowers

Shad

Hemlocks

Circular Stairway

Deck

Fig. 6–8.

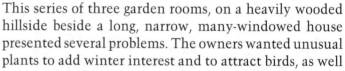

0   5   10

This series of three garden rooms, on a heavily wooded hillside beside a long, narrow, many-windowed house presented several problems. The owners wanted unusual plants to add winter interest and to attract birds, as well as space for spring flowers and a small pool which could be viewed from the kitchen.

It was necessary to remove five trees to open up the area and provide better light for the gardens. The steep, awkward slope outside the low basement windows had to be regraded. Natural fieldstones were available, so they were used for the walls. No footings are necessary for this kind of dry wall which can move with the heaving and thawing of the ground.

The three garden rooms serve quite different purposes. The lowest one below the deck is useful for boat storage, a potting bench, boots, skis, and the like. The next garden above, a twenty-by-thirty-foot rectangle, is called the "Pausing Garden," and is approached from the deck by a spiral staircase (these come in various sizes to fit into small areas). There is a low sitting wall and water feature in the corner. The pool with water splashing over rocks as it falls from above makes a nice view from the kitchen window and is something the birds enjoy daily.

The third garden is almost square, thirty-two by thirty-five feet, and is approached by several steps. Here there is space for flowers along the retaining wall and by the low windows of the basement. Low hollies and white azaleas along the outside wall with a weeping hemlock in the corner by the pool complete this picture.

Fig. 6–9.

**A LONG NARROW
GARDEN**

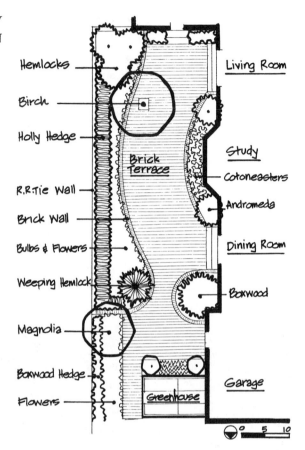

Hemlocks
Birch
Holly Hedge
Brick Terrace
R.R.Tie Wall
Brick Wall
Bulbs & Flowers
Weeping Hemlock
Magnolia
Boxwood Hedge
Flowers

Living Room
Study
Cotoneasters
Andromeda
Dining Room
Boxwood
Garage
Greenhouse

0   5   10

Fig. 6–10.

A small suburban homesite had doors from a bedroom,
living room, and dining room opening on to a long narrow garden twenty-five by sixty feet. A town ordinance
prevented high walls or fences, but we were allowed to
build a double wall three feet high and plant inside this
in order to create privacy from the neighboring house.

The straight back wall along the property line is
made of railroad ties and serves as a retaining wall. The
front wall of brick with long curved ends tends to widen
the entire area, as does the low sitting wall below the
picture window. One birch tree was placed strategically
outside the living room door, also giving privacy to the

bedroom wing. It is a multiple stem white birch with soft feathery foliage throughout the summer and nice winter color in the bark. Plantings include a hedge of Japanese holly and hemlocks at the edge of the wall. Cotoneasters in two varieties fill the bed below the windows.

The tulips give abundance of color for a long time in the spring, then are lifted and given to friends to be replanted each fall with new ones. Annuals are changed each year from seedlings grown in the greenhouse.

Fig. 6-11.

A SIDE GARDEN

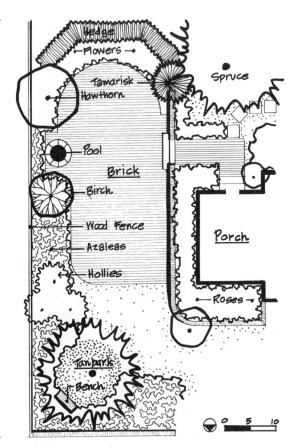

Fig. 6–12.

An area thirty-five by fifty feet at the side of a suburban home has been developed into a large brick terrace which was laid by the owners over a period of several years. They did the construction work in intervals between sailing and traveling and all the other things they liked to do. Now that it is finished this delightful garden has become a vital, constantly used part of their lives, and makes the long months of work seem highly worthwhile.

An interesting enclosed porch was added to the house so the owners could see the garden and enjoy it all winter. With the encircling beds of evergreens there is always something attractive to look at, and the birch tree with its white bark lends a quiet charm in winter.

In the summer, flower borders are filled with peonies and iris, followed later by phlox, delphinium, and lilies. Annuals raised from seed include blue ageratum, yellow marigolds, snaps, and zinnias, and celosia which is a long-lasting annual.

The Brown Jordan furniture in pale green is particularly attractive against the red brick. Notice in this picture (Fig. 6–14) the tamarix with its pale pink flowers and yellow centers and the curved bed of flowers leading to the pool where old Mr. Owl welcomes you to his domain, the real feature of this garden.

Beneath an old evergreen tree on the north a little tanbark path is outlined with heather and beckons you to pause for a final view of the garden.

Fig. 6–13.

**AN EVERGREEN
GARDEN**

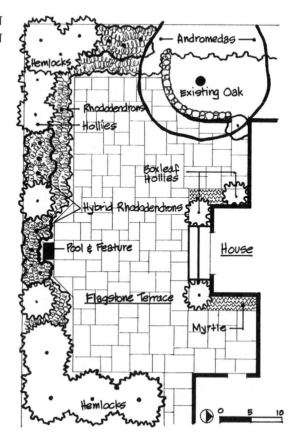

Fig. 6–14.

A suburban garden twenty-five by sixty feet whose long-est dimension runs at right angles to the house presented certain problems. There was little chance to create a long vista from the main approach of the living room. So the garden feature, a small fountain, was placed opposite a new glass-walled room recently added to the house. Extending on each side are paved areas for dining and relaxing. Thus, the narrow backyard was given a greater feeling of space, allowing comfortable outdoor living and requiring little maintenance.

Since the garden gets little sunshine, planting included hemlocks for a background and rhododendrons—Boule de Neige, Roseum elegans, and Mrs. C. S. Sargent.

Andromeda used near the house with low hollies on each side of the door complete the evergreen planting. The existing oak tree to the right of the house was on a higher level, so it was necessary to build a dry stone wall around it which also acts as a sitting wall. Tucked in among the evergreens in summer white impatiens is planted for its long flowering, adaptability to shade, and attractiveness at night.

Fig. 6–15.

A DRY STREAM
ON A HILLSIDE

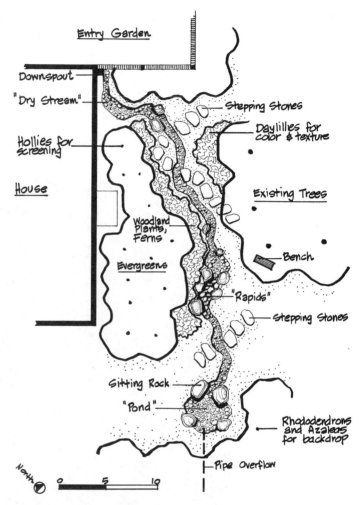

Entry Garden

Downspout

"Dry Stream"

Stepping Stones

Daylilies for color & texture

Hollies for screening

House

Existing Trees

Woodland Plants, Ferns

Evergreens

Bench

"Rapids"

Stepping Stones

Sitting Rock

"Pond"

Rhododendrons and Azaleas for backdrop

Pipe Overflow

North

0   5   10

Fig. 6–16.

Rainwater runoff from this house on a fairly steep hill-side was an eyesore as well as a maintenance problem. Originally, the downspout water ran from the corner of the house down a slope dropping one foot for every five in a muddy gulch. Then for a while a green precast concrete trough was used to drain this water in a long straight channel down the fifty feet of hillside. When something more imaginative was requested, the solution of a rocky stream bed was worked out. Meandering in a leisurely way down the hillside the stream bed not only solves the problem of rushing water after each rain, but also makes an attractive garden feature all the rest of the time.

An eighteen-inch trough was dug following the plan for the dry stream and this was lined with stones two to five inches in size. If subsoil has a lot of clay in it, a four-inch cushion of sand should be used. Larger stepping stones were placed along this stream as an invitation to saunter back and forth. Since this was a very woodsy area, plants such as ferns, violets, iris cristata, May apple, hosta, liriope, Solomon's seal, bergenia, and sweet woodruff were carefully chosen to cover the bank and creep along one edge of the stream. The other side is open lawn.

Fig. 6–17.

A HILLSIDE FLOWER GARDEN

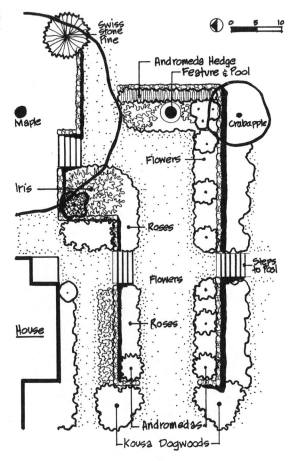

Swiss Stone Pine

Andromeda Hedge
Feature & Pool

Maple

Crabapple

Flowers

Iris

Roses

Steps to Pool

Flowers

House

Roses

Andromedas

Kousa Dogwoods

Fig. 6-18.

Graded in such a way as to make a level area sixty feet long on the hillside next to the house, this garden makes a perfect place for growing roses, iris, spring bulbs, and chrysanthemums. It is only sixteen feet wide with a grass path down the center and four-foot beds on each side. The roses against the wall were selected to stand the severe conditions of this northern climate. Most of the iris in the corners are unusual varieties and make a fine display in early June. A fragrant viburnum in one corner gives lovely color and perfumes the air in the early spring.

Since this garden is only enjoyed in the spring and fall, the roses are cut back hard in late July and fed, so that they will give glorious bloom all fall. An edging of sweet alyssum seed has been planted along the border, but had not yet come up when the picture was taken. Its bloom and fragrance last well into October.

The border on the north with its two-foot stone wall has andromeda spaced ten feet apart to give rhythm to this long bed as well as winter interest. Here the spring bulbs are the important feature with a border of pansies in selected colors.

Fig. 6–19.

A FLOWER PATTERN GARDEN

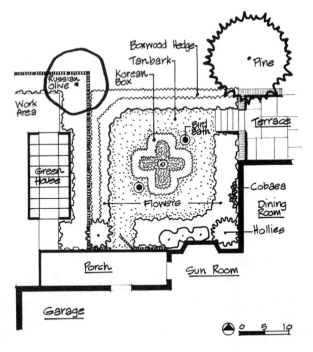

Fig. 6–20.

A pattern garden is a delight. To walk around the beds can be a pleasurable experience. Shown here is a twenty-five-by-twenty-nine-foot area, developed a few years ago and designed to be viewed from the terrace, dining room, plant room, and greenhouse.

It was necessary to have the foundation of evergreen material for year-round interest. The center area, with its Korean box hedge (all grown from cuttings) and grey santolina, looks attractive summer or winter. In front of the outer boxwood hedge is a small bed filled with flowers throughout the season—coral bell, white alyssum, several varieties of thyme, lemon drop marigolds, blue ageratum, lamb's ears, coral salvia, tobacco plant, delicate lacy dusty miller, and begonias for the shady areas.

Clematis is slowly climbing over the fence with cobea and moon flowers which are fast annual growers.

Garden features, collected on travels, are positioned where they can be viewed from the windows and terrace. Large tubs of begonias and gray dusty miller on the steps carry the color theme.

This garden requires considerable care, but for people who love to garden and do all the work of preparation, propagating, and planting, it is a joy. Once planted, with the annuals for the summer added to the existing perennial plants and evergreens, mulching reduces much of the work of weeding and watering.

Designed by owner.

Fig. 6–21.

AN HERB GARDEN

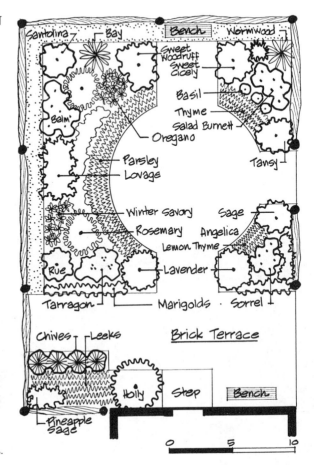

Fig. 6–22.

For a house built recently in the Williamsburg style an enclosed herb garden, thirty by twenty-two feet, was placed near the kitchen door. Herbs are used constantly by the family and this flat open space was the most convenient setting.

Enclosed with a two-rail fence, the garden has a walk around the outside of crushed clam shells and a circular bricked area in the center. A tiny brick terrace adjacent to the back door is used for drying herbs and also as a place for cleaning fish caught in the waters below.

The center is bordered with parsley and thyme. The other herbs include chives, savory, dill, sage, sweet cicily, lavender, and lemon verbena. All are growing extremely well in this sunny spot as they had good soil preparation before planting, and their spicy fragrance wafts delightfully into the house.

Fig. 6–23.

TWO DECK GARDENS

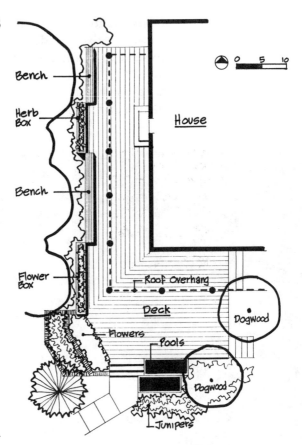

Fig. 6–24.

Decks can be conceived as the only garden room, especially when the rest of the property is woodland, meadow, or marshland. On these two sites there was no place else to plant, so the decks had to be planned with adequate containers for year-round variety—evergreens for the winter, flowers for the summer.

In this case, the ground sloped sharply from the house, and the existing porch and wall were too narrow for really enjoyable outdoor life. The new deck, some twelve feet wider, was laid over the existing flagstone porch and provided with planters and benches. At one end two plastic pools, one below the other, add the pleasant sound of water, as well as making an interesting foreground for the meadows beyond.

Fig. 6–25.

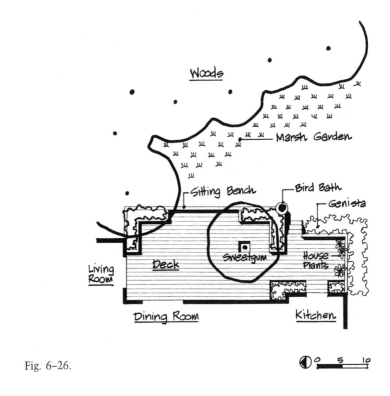

Fig. 6–26.

On another site the deck overlooks woodlands along salt water marshes and was designed as an outdoor room and garden. Containers were built along part of the deck and create two different rooms—one near the kitchen for dining and the other off the dining room and living room for relaxing. A large sweetgum tree was planted in an opening of this deck to provide the roots with plenty of space to grow naturally. Around it are artemisia and cotoneasters. The large wooden boxes have some junipers to give color in the winter along with annuals for the summer.

Fig. 6–27.

AN ENTRANCE GARDEN

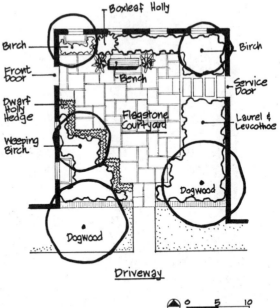

Fig. 6–28.

An entrance area twenty by eighteen feet within the wings of a house led to a main corner door. Previously there had been a narrow path through a small grass plot, not very appropriate to the size and architecture of the house. This was completely changed. The grass was removed, the center area paved, the planting rearranged. A handsome wrought iron bench was placed opposite the gate as a welcome note, with pots of geraniums around it. These changes gave dignity and year-round color to the entrance of this stately house.

Birches to frame the door, on one side a clump of white birch and on the other a weeping birch, were planted along with low hollies to accent the pattern.

Besides making guests feel welcome, this little garden can also be used as a sheltered sitting terrace where one can enjoy a cup of tea on chilly days.

Fig. 6–29.

Fig. 6–30.

**AN OVERGROWN
GARDEN REVAMPED**

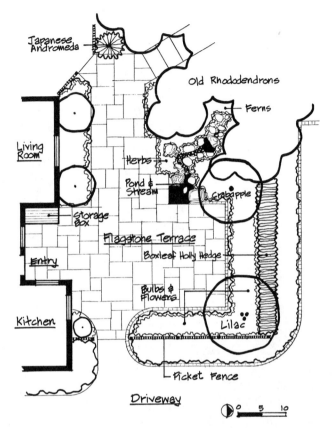

Japanese Andromeda

Old Rhododendrons

Ferns

Living Room

Herbs

Pond & Stream

Crabapple

Storage Box

Flagstone Terrace

Boxleaf Holly Hedge

Entry

Bulbs & Flowers

Kitchen

Lilac

Picket Fence

Driveway

Fig. 6–31.

The flagstone terrace of an old colonial house at the foot of a hill was originally in fairly good condition. However, a wall of tall rhododendrons so overshadowed the garden that some had to be removed and others pruned to create a more open feeling. A lilac and crab apple were allowed to emerge and make an interesting form above.

The terrace was extended and granite-block curbing used to give it a more defined form with a protected spot for house plants, a bird bath, and bird feeders. A picket fence, in keeping with the colonial house, and a holly hedge separate the garden from the driveway and provide a backdrop for flowers and bulbs.

Most importantly, a little brook and pool were added as a focal point. A recirculating water system was installed in the existing slope, so that the water appears to be coming out of a spring and splashing down a natural stream to the pool. The birds enjoy it for they have water, food, and shelter, and it is a delightful place to sit while you watch and listen.

What is important in remodeling an old garden is to save any unusual existing plants, trim back others, and add a personal touch of your own.

Designed by owner.

Fig. 6–32.

A TREE GARDEN

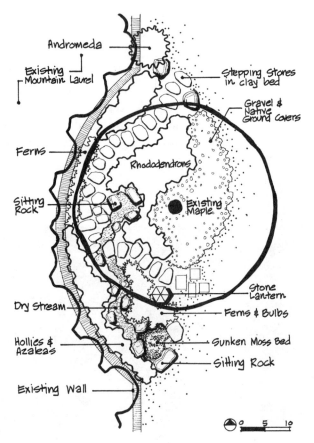

Andromeda

Existing Mountain Laurel

Stepping Stones in clay bed

Gravel & Native Ground Covers

Ferns

Rhododendrons

Sitting Rock

Existing Maple

Dry Stream

Stone Lantern

Ferns & Bulbs

Hollies & Azaleas

Sunken Moss Bed

Sitting Rock

Existing Wall

Fig. 6–33.

In this country garden a large old red maple grew from a mound three feet higher than the grass area around it. In order to include this in the garden treatment, as it was visible from a pool terrace, the grassy earth behind the tree was built up even higher and a stepping-stone walk around it was laid in the Japanese manner. Starting on the right, the path wanders up over the mound where wild flowers from the woods, Solomon's seal, partridge berry, wintergreen, ground pine, and Canada mayflower were planted.

As the path neared the top, a few laurel and fragrant azaleas were added beneath old white pines on the other side of the wall. The path descends through dwarf rhododendrons, azaleas, and creeping cotoneaster.

In a small hollow at the bottom of the slope a sunken moss bed was built using large native stones. An old Japanese stone lantern makes an exotic but appropriate feature amidst ajuga and three varieties of ferns—Cinnamon, New York, and Interrupted.

Fig. 6–34.

**A ROCKY LEDGE
GARDEN**

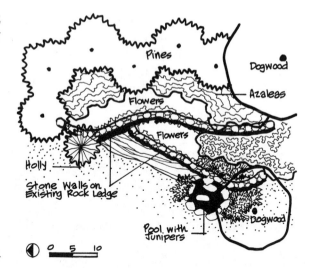

Fig. 6–35.

An outcrop of rock hardly seems a likely place for a garden but here it was important to make one as the rock faced the family room and was very visible from the new terrace.

Two separate walls were built taking advantage of the exposed rock which forms a pleasant curve. The upper level has space for some flowers but is planted predominately with white azaleas, dwarf rhododendrons, and hollies. A background of pines hides the neighbor's garage. The second wall nestling into the rock at a lower level is filled with flowers and ends at the pool.

This pool, as the focal feature, built up and bordered with rocks looks so natural that the birds have adopted it as their own. Junipers growing over the edge and trailing plants filling the crevices make this a delightful garden for all to enjoy throughout the year.

Fig. 6–36.

AN EARLY SPRING GARDEN

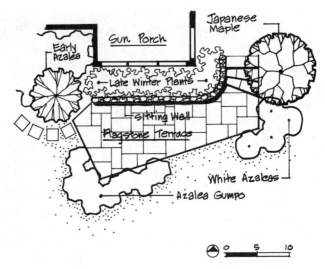

Fig. 6–37.

An open porch enclosed to make an indoor plant room provided space just outside for a special little garden. With a low sitting wall, the same material as the house, built four feet out from the porch there was ample space for early spring blooming plants.

Below this a flagstone terrace angled to make space for several to sit comfortably is approached by two steps from the porch. Beneath the branches of an old gnarled Japanese maple tree this little terrace makes a sheltered spot for late winter and spring sunning.

In the raised bed, flowering plum is espaliered against the wall with low rhododendrons (Purple Gem and Ramapo with gray-green leaves and violet flowers). A few yellow blooming Keiskei, native mountain andromeda, and taller native azaleas grow at the end of the bed.

In between the low shrubs are crocus, snowdrops, scillas, winter aconite, and small tulips (Clusiana and Kaufmanniana).

Fig. 6–38.

A COTTAGE GARDEN

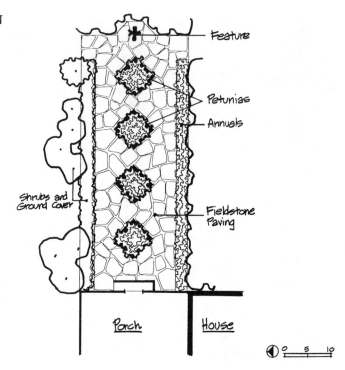

Feature

Petunias

Annuals

Shrubs and
Ground Cover

Fieldstone
Paving

Porch   House

Fig. 6–39.

The back lot of a New England seashore cottage was transformed into a pattern garden with a wooden swan as the focal point.

The four square beds are filled with petunias and angled toward the porch to create a colorful summer perspective. Beds of snapdragons and other summer-blooming annuals flank the paved area with ground cover and petunia borders. Walks of random native flagstone laid dry keep the rustic cottage feeling.

Designed by MARION COFFIN, *L.A.*

Fig. 6–40.

Detail Planning

7 practical guides to garden details

In the previous plans you have seen how important it is to design your garden thoughtfully and include what you and your family want—to create an attractive outdoor room. Remember it is more economical to have as many elements as possible laid out on paper in advance so that you can estimate costs before you start digging, constructing, and planting.

THE APPROACH TO YOUR GARDEN

Many of these ideas will apply either to a city or a country home, but let's think first about how to get into your garden if it is in the city.

Remodeled brownstones and town houses nowadays are very often divided into apartments. Thus the main living rooms can be either above or below the garden, needing steps of some kind to the outdoor living area. Iron, wood, brick, or concrete are the usual materials. These steps should have an easy riser (four to five inches high) and a wide tread (twelve to fifteen inches). The steps should be in keeping with the architectural style as well as affording comfortable access even when glasses and dishes are being carried back and forth.

The step width depends upon the scale of the yard. If it is pract' l, steps five feet wide make for a gracious way up and down. If you can't spare the five feet, try to make them at least three feet wide. The platform just outside the door ought to extend three feet to provide space to pause comfortably.

If there is an old door on the basement level but none on the first floor, as is often the case, it may mean changing a window into a door and providing proper security that is permanent and good looking. Lighting for doors and steps should also be designed at this time with adequate outlets so that outdoor fixtures may be installed.

Figs. 7–1 through 7–6 show various solutions to the problem of this first step into the garden. If you are working with an architect on the house remodeling be sure to ask about sturdy doors to the garden, windows, and security devices.

Sliding doors are available in wood or aluminum, single or double, plate glass or thermal. Metal is about

Fig. 7–1. Two four-foot French doors in this Georgian house allow access to the brick-paved garden. In summer when the doors are left open, screens could be installed. French doors can be ordered up to six feet wide and are customarily made of wood and glass, but can also be made of metal and glass of varying thicknesses.

Fig. 7–2. In remodeling this brownstone a young couple with three children decided to make the kitchen into their family room. Sliding glass doors were put in at the same level as the kitchen floor to give easy access into the garden. The cost of such an installation while renovation is underway is not excessive. These sliding glass doors, thirty inches wide, can be pushed entirely into the wall since there is sufficient space for slots on each side. Be sure that the paving directly outside is set in cement two feet beyond the door, and that there is a pitch of at least one-eighth inch per foot away from the door to provide for proper drainage.

Fig. 7–3. Many city houses have a small porch or landing on the first floor. A durable and inexpensive open stairway with rough-surface iron treads three feet wide and a simple metal railing has been constructed here to provide easy descent to the garden.

Fig. 7–4. For either city or country houses the elegant curves of a spiral staircase make a decorative and convenient passage between the garden and the first or second stories. In addition to saving space, spirals are rugged and reliable, adaptable to modern or traditional buildings, and available in one-piece welded construction for easy installation. Spirals come left- or right-handed, in various diameters, and in practically any height.

the same price as wood but more satisfactory since it slides more easily. The overall width could vary from five to eight feet, and the height from the standard six feet two inches to six feet ten inches. Any door made to order takes considerable time and costs a great deal more.

The country home usually has several doors leading out to the garden area. One of these should have a direct approach to the newly designed garden. If it is only a short drop below the house, then you can use the open type of steps which are easier to build and much less expensive than masonry.

You may choose a spiral stairway for reasons of space and form. One is shown here that gives quick and easy access to the ground from an upper floor. Even the pet poodle finally learned how to maneuver on it.

Fig. 7–5. Three sturdy plank steps descend to this paved terrace from a platform six feet wide and four feet deep outside the double door. This is a simple, comfortable, and low-cost solution. See-through steps look airy, while their width obviates the need for a handrail.

Fig. 7–6. In an old townhouse the rear kitchen was remodeled for present-day living into a garden room. This room opens on to a small deck through six-foot-wide sliding glass doors. The deck, made as small as feasible so as not to take up the whole extent of the rear façade, makes an easy approach to the garden below.

TERRACES
AND DECKS

Terraces

The second guide point to consider in developing your garden details should be the type of paving material and pattern you intend to use. There are the usual flagstone, brick, concrete, or gravel but there are also other materials on the market which lend themselves extremely well to paving small gardens. Brick or concrete pavers come in many shapes and colors and can be used for unusual effects. In the city you will have the problem of transporting the materials through the house from the street to your garden area. This is heavy work and will take considerable time but once you have finished your garden floor it will be worth the effort for it will be practical and easy to keep clean.

Perhaps there was an existing walk (as in all nineteenth-century gardens) made of old flagstones or bricks and if so, be sure to dig them up and save them. Even the stone curbing can be useful for dry walls or relaid as a new curb.

Design the floor pattern of your garden so that it will have an interesting texture and color, reduce maintenance, and be attractive throughout the year.

Bricks are easy to use, of good color and small scale, and you have a wide variety of patterns to choose from—running bond, herringbone, or basket weave (see Fig. 7–7). Sometimes it is fun to use more than one pattern, especially if the garden is large and you want to show a change of direction.

If you have decided on brick paving, consider the various designs that lend themselves to this material. For those who do it themselves, brick is much easier to lay than flagstone. For estimating purposes figure for 100 square feet, 500 bricks and nine cubic yards of sand.

In a shady area bricks often become very dark and lose their color so they will need to be cleaned. Use muriatic acid (follow instructions), a stiff brush, and hard

Fig. 7–7.

Running Bond

Basket Weave

Herringbone

Fig. 7–8.

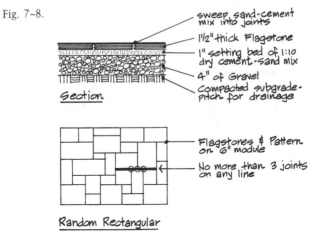

sweep sand-cement mix into joints

1½" thick Flagstone

1" setting bed of 1:10 dry cement-sand mix

4" of Gravel

Compacted subgrade-pitch for drainage

Section

Flagstones & Pattern on 6" module

No more than 3 joints on any line

Random Rectangular

scrubbing. This, however, will also remove any moss that may be growing.

Flagstone or bluestone comes in cut pieces which are usually available at stoneyards. If you get the flagstone in rectangular pieces from one to four feet, you can use a pattern that the stoneyard will prepare for you. Extra-large slabs, or any stone cut to a curve, will cost

Fig. 7–9. In this rectangular flagstone paving the pattern is regular but appears interestingly random. The bed is four inches of crushed stone plus two inches of sand into which stones are pressed with tight joints. Plants here are pinks and low juniper, which like to spread out over the stone.

Fig. 7–10. To break up a large expanse of paving, creeping thyme with its pink flowers and pungent spicy smell, has been planted between joints. Only a few inches need to be scraped out of joints, and a mixture of topsoil and peat moss inserted. Seed can be used, or small plants pinned down with common hairpins. This shows two-year growth.

In the corner by the wall where two flagstones were removed, cotoneaster has been planted to spread out in a fan shape. Pink geraniums give added color in this corner.

more. The irregular stones are hard to use and even harder to walk on unless you intend to fill in the uneven joints with sand or creeping plants.

Patio blocks which are made of concrete come in various colors and can be laid to a pattern. This is less expensive than brick or flagstone. Exposed aggregate, which is concrete mixed with stones so that there is a textured surface, can also be attractive.

Fig. 7–11. Gravel beside the greenhouse is practical where there is much traffic, and where plants are set out for the summer. The stepping-stones are laid in a curve so that they almost touch on one side and are further apart on the outside.

Fig. 7–12. These bricks in a herringbone pattern are laid on end rather than flat and give a different texture to a terrace. Note the border of brick, the brick pool and the curb for the raised beds.

Designed by MARION COFFIN, L.A.

Gravel is the least expensive paving material and can often be used as a temporary measure while you decide where to put permanent planting islands or zones, or it can form part of the definite design. Size of gravel must be chosen carefully as larger stones tend to move under the feet but this can be used to advantage to slow up the pace of walking. Very fine gravel such as screenings will become compacted and provide a hard surface. Gravel should be two inches thick and have a sheet of polyethylene (with a few holes for drainage)

Fig. 7–13. Brick laid in different ways adds a warm color note to any garden. It is easy and fun to do yourself. Here running-bond has been laid on a bed of gravel and sand. Outside brick edging should be set in cement so terrace and walk will not push out owing to heaving and thawing. Note how you can change the pattern of brick to make a connection between terrace and door.

beneath it to prevent weeds. Gravel between a curb and a fountain, for example, or around sculptures, is pleasantly combined with other paving materials.

I have usually recommended laying flagstone or brick on a two-inch sand cushion under which there should be some porous material such as gravel or crushed stone to a depth of four inches (see Fig. 7–8). This provides the necessary drainage so that winter heaving will not be damaging. Flagstone varies in thickness from one inch to two inches. The thicker stones will be better because they are heavier and will not crack as readily as the thin stones. Be sure to buy rectangular pieces with shadings of color that are pleasing. It is often advisable to mix sand and dry cement (one part of cement to ten parts of sand) to ensure firm joints and prevent weeds or moss from coming up through the joints.

City Gardens

PLATE 1.   Studio Garden. Hanging baskets
and a bronze sculpture in one corner of
an eleven-by-twenty-four-foot area (chapter 3).

PLATE 2 (left). Square Garden. Espaliered Japanese holly growing against wood fence with flowers in a sunny, brick-paved garden (chapter 3).

PLATE 3 (below). Rectangular Garden. An old silver maple casts a shadow on the brick paving and raised beds (chapter 3).

PLATE 4 (right). Victorian Garden. Three-tiered fountain has Korean box and Kaufmanniana tulips planted nearby (chapter 3).

PLATE 5 (Opposite). Long Narrow Garden. Along a curving flagstone walk connecting two terraces are plantings of rhododendron, ground cover, and flowers (chapter 3).

PLATE 6 (left). Garden and Parking Area. Sliding doors open from the street for parking. Paving continues into the sitting space, surrounded by low evergreens (chapter 3).

PLATE 7 (below). Shallow Garden. Fleecevine trained on a white fence. Vertical interest is provided by clump of small birches (chapter 3).

PLATE 8 (left).   Pattern Garden.
Lombardy poplars hide building at rear.
Center circle is planted with begonias,
pattern beds with ivy (chapter 3).

PLATE 9 (below).   Historic Garden. Blue
and white scillas in pattern beds, cottage
tulips against the fence with ivy trained
on it in a diamond pattern (chapter 3).

PLATE 10 (right).   Oval Garden. An old
saucer magnolia blooming in a gravel bed
set off by hollies and azaleas (chapter 3).

PLATE 11 and 12. Two views of a city garden, showing wisteria-covered porch, and small lawn with picket fence.

Country Gardens

PLATE 13.   Garden with Waterfalls. In the
shade of a maple tree, rocks and water give
sound and texture to a corner terrace

PLATE 14 (left). Garden Terrace with View. Cardinal tulips are one of seasonally changing blooms in beds next to St. Francis statue, looking out to hills beyond pond and woods (chapter 6).

PLATE 15 (below). Long Narrow Garden. Curving brick walls hold hemlock and flower beds and lead the eye toward the brick-based greenhouse (chapter 6).

PLATE 16 (right). Dry Stream Hillside. Created to correct a rainwater drainage problem, the stream became an attractive garden feature even when dry (chapter 6).

PLATE 17 (left). Rocky Ledge Garden. Walls creating two
planting areas were built on existing rock outcrop (chapter 6).

PLATE 18 (above). Flower Pattern Garden. Center pattern
with clipped box hedge and santolina retains color all year
round. Outer border shows seasonal flowers (chapter 6).

PLATE 19 (below). Natural Boulders. Huge stones left in
place with planting crevices for unusual dwarf evergreens.
Designed by Edwin F. Steffek.

PLATE 20 (above left). A summer border filled with annuals and perennials giving constant bloom for four months.

PLATE 21 (below left). A wide border of daylilies blooms for two summer months near the sea, backed by Japanese black pines.

PLATE 22 (right). A lead wood-nymph figure makes a fountain feature with its pie-shaped lead pool set in the corner of a terrace.

PLATE 23 (below). Cornelian cherry makes a pleasant shadow on the lawn. In front of old laurels is a four-foot border for summer blooms.

PLATE 24 (above).   An old Japanese maple provides the setting for an antique lantern and dipping well.

PLATE 25 (below).   Heaths and heathers planted between carefully placed rocks bloom from spring into late winter. Behind is a hedge of mountain laurel.

Decks I used to think decks were too contemporary to belong with most older houses and that a garden at ground level with proper access was more enjoyable, but I have discovered how useful decks can be and what a good alter-

Fig. 7–14. Sliding glass doors open on to a deck used for dining which extends over rocks and little waterfalls. Water running below the deck drops to a small pool. The largest rock is a stepping-stone to the lower terrace.

Fig. 7–15. Adjacent to the kitchen of a city house, the small railed deck makes an ideal spot for morning coffee or summer suppers, and for house plants to summer out. Access to the yard is from the deck, with storage space below.

Fig. 7–16. This deck lets outdoor living space flow out and down to the terrain. The pools are of black vinyl with wooden copings. Brick paving and railroad-tie steps make a gentle curve and natural boulders have been left in place.

native choice they are for the garden floor, giving a spacious feeling to the house and making fine safe places for children.

Owing to the terrain at the seaside or in the mountains, a deck is sometimes the only way to create a garden room. A vacation home or ski lodge deck can offer the advantage of views unobtainable from the house or give the wonderful feeling of sitting in the tree tops and is perfect for sunbathing and outdoor living.

There are a great many ways to build a deck, as well as many materials to use—redwood, cedar, cypress, or fir, weathered to soft gray, or stained and textured to blend with the house and its site. The boards can be laid parallel to the house or in other patterns depending on structure below. It is also possible to buy prepared sections which can be put together in squares, either diamond or parquet, like indoor flooring. A strong frame is needed and generally two-by-sixes are spaced sixteen inches apart to support the surface boards. These can be two-by-threes or two-by-fours in various lengths, and should have a small space between them for drainage.

Decks break the barriers between indoors and outdoors, especially with sliding glass doors. Since water never stays on decks, they can be used again right after a rain and require little maintenance compared to the constant care a garden should receive. Deck seats and planting containers can be permanent parts of the basic design, or portable for seasonal use and changing arrangement.

GARDEN STEPS, RAMPS, AND PATHS

If your garden is on different levels, it is a challenge to design steps or ramps which will be unusual and attractive as well as safe and easy to use. Moving from one level to another inside the garden presents different problems from those mentioned earlier in dealing with the approach to the garden from the house.

The grades within the garden will have been determined, so you know that one end is, for example, two or three feet lower. In this case, steps can be built with a cheek wall that extends the whole length of the slope, or they can be built into one section of the bank with planting on each side. If the house is of brick, it would be appropriate to have a low brick wall with brick steps, but there can be many variations, as can be seen in the figures. Stone, either dry or on a foundation, railroad ties, concrete blocks, or poured concrete are some suggestions (Fig. 7–17). To plan a proper and comfortable outdoor step, low risers and wide treads are needed. Anything from a four-inch riser to six inches is satisfactory, and the tread should be fourteen to eighteen inches (Fig. 7–18). My own favorite is a five-inch riser and a sixteen-inch tread.

Ramps are useful where there is a gradual slope, or where a rustic woodsy appearance is desired (Fig. 7–19). Also, ramps may be needed where there are elderly peo-

Fig. 7–17.

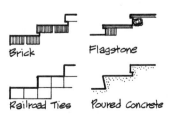

Brick   Flagstone

Railroad Ties   Poured Concrete

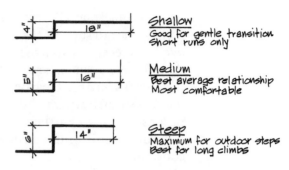

Shallow
Good for gentle transition
Short runs only

Medium
Best average relationship
Most comfortable

Steep
Maximum for outdoor steps
Best for long climbs

Fig. 7–18.

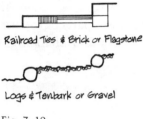

Railroad Ties & Brick or Flagstone

Logs & Tanbark or Gravel

Fig. 7–19.

ple, wheelchairs, baby carriages, or small children, or simply for wheeling tea wagons or portable barbecues.

A step-ramp should have a six-inch riser and a six-foot tread, with a slight forward pitch on the tread. This allows the walker to take three steps on each tread. The

Fig. 7–20. Here railroad-tie steps were used to climb eight and a half feet in a limited space. Therefore it was necessary to turn the steps twice in order to have a span long enough to maintain proper height of risers. Note that two ties were placed parallel on each tread as one alone is not broad enough to support the walker's foot.

Fig. 7–21. Six-foot-wide field-stone steps with level cheek wall, six-inch risers, and fourteen-inch treads make an easy transition between two terraces. The steps are made of carefully fitted stones from the site on a concrete foundation.

Designed by JAMES S. KENNEDY.

material can be railroad ties with tanbark chips, flagstone, brick, concrete, or weatherproofed wood.

Paths are an important part of garden design, not only for circulation but also to give the effect of a wider or longer area—to create perspective. A grass path lead-

Fig. 7–22. From a porch a brick path leads a few paces to these steps, constructed on a concrete foundation, with treads sixteen inches wide and risers of six inches. The projection of the step, one and a half inches, makes what is known as the nose and gives a nice shadow line to the step.

Fig. 7–23. In a city yard access to a small lawn area above the lower terrace was created with a curving step-ramp of brick. Ivy and cotoneasters have been trained over the low concrete cheek wall.

Fig. 7–24. Railroad ties eight feet wide, the usual size of old ties (new ones can be cut to any size you wish) make a simple ramp that is easy to build. Soft wood chips were used between the ties for an easy, low-maintenance tread. Cotoneaster and myrtle with spring bulbs cover the bank.

Fig. 7–25. Flagstones, two inches thick and at least two feet square are laid with four to six inches of mulch or gravel between them. Stepping-stones laid in this manner can easily be formed into a curve to follow the direction of a path. Simply place them in the way you wish to walk and then pick them up and cut out the soil beneath. Where ground is low or the water table high it may be advisable to put a gravel base below each stone.

ing from a terrace becomes an irresistible invitation to stroll out into the garden.

Paths should be at least three feet wide, but can be as wide as the space and design permit. Materials can be brick, stone, woodchips, gravel, or any other paving material. Be sure to prepare the ground properly so that it has an adequate pitch and will not allow ruts and puddles to form.

A tip on dealing with weeds and crab grass: mix the coarse salt used for snow removal or ice-cream freezers into a thick solution and pour carefully into cracks. This will kill off other plants as well as weeds, so be sure not to pour it on path borders or planted areas.

WALLS AND FENCES Garden enclosures have many purposes—to protect from any outside access, to screen, to shelter from wind, to create intimacy, to serve purely as decoration, or to support vines. Many city brownstones already have fences around their backyards, and if in good condition can spare you a rather large expense. However, brick or

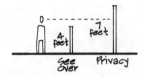

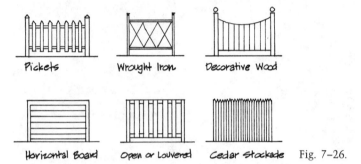

Fig. 7-26.

stone walls give a very special feeling to a backyard and make a more intimate garden enclosure.

Masonry construction is extremely costly as walls need a footing. Its extent depends upon climate and the depth to which frost penetrates. Be sure in a northern climate that the footing goes below the frost line in order to prevent any wall section from heaving.

If the expense of a masonry wall is prohibitive, consider designing a fence or purchasing one of the prefabricated ones. Fence posts should be set in concrete to prevent rotting, and cypress or redwood used for durability. Locust is excellent for posts; white cedar or Douglas fir are cheaper, but do not last as long. Posts must always be treated with a wood preservative.

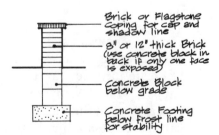

Fig. 7-27.

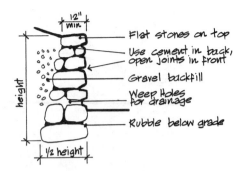

Fig. 7–28.

In some places where neighbors share backyard and garden areas, fences are eliminated in order to provide an open and spacious feeling. In such cases, a low hedge can be used to enclose each family's private sitting or dining space.

Before planning for a fence, be sure to check your town or city regulations to verify that you are allowed to build a fence and the maximum permissible height.

Fences and walls should be part of the overall garden design. Fences can be post and rail, picket, board, or chain link. Post-and-rail fences are easily installed and make excellent boundaries with planting and vines. Nowadays there is a great variety of pickets, which are always in keeping with Colonial-style homes.

A solid board fence, whether horizontal, vertical, or louvered, can be designed in almost any height to fit your needs. The prefab ones are easy to install, but they lack variety and often are not very ornamental so they need to be vine-covered or masked by shrubbery.

Fences are also practical if you want to disguise an entrance. By overlapping each section and leaving three or four feet between them, a workable and attractive passway is created into and out of your garden.

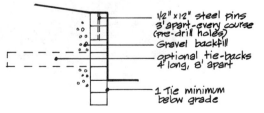

Fig. 7–29.

Fig. 7–30. A pierced brick wall is another way of encircling a garden. Here, a sitting wall eight inches thick and two feet high has been used with a two-inch flagstone coping.

Interior walls, whether free-standing or retaining, must also be designed as part of the basic garden plan. Walls can be used to divide the area, perhaps separating two levels as in Figure 7–32, or to set off flower, vegetable, and herb gardens. Barbecues can be built into walled

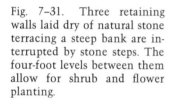

Fig. 7–31. Three retaining walls laid dry of natural stone terracing a steep bank are interrupted by stone steps. The four-foot levels between them allow for shrub and flower planting.

Fig. 7–32.   A brick wall between two garden levels serves also as a sitting wall. Notice the weep holes which should always be made to allow water to trickle through.

nooks, and low walls around trees make charming shady sitting places.

A sitting wall provides additional space in your garden for entertaining all year round. It can be useful for an array of potted plants or even for feeding birds. I know of one low wall in a southern garden where sunflower seed is put out daily for the cardinals. Watching the birds feeding on the old brick wall in late afternoon light has become a delightful family appointment.

Even a low wall (Fig. 7–27), whether of brick, stone, or concrete, must have a footing or foundation well

Fig. 7–33. Railroad ties used to make a raised bed just below a high porch for safety as well as planting. This is an inexpensive way to build a low retaining wall, and looks well with junipers growing over the edges.

below the frost line. The flat stone coping on top should extend at least a half inch on either side so that it is wide enough to sit on comfortably. Two inches is the recommended minimum thickness.

A retaining wall, designed to create one or more level areas on a slope, can be constructed of many kinds of stone or brick, or of inexpensive railroad ties (Fig. 7–29). If a retaining wall (Fig. 7–28) is laid dry against a slope or bank, you will need to lay a stone base eight to ten inches below ground level. This dry stone retaining wall may be three feet high, but any higher could get you into trouble. If the slope is higher, move back a few feet and build a second retaining wall.

Hollow cement blocks in various sizes (eight by

Fig. 7–34. A dry stone wall can also be designed so that rock plants will grow between the crevices. Here alyssum and sedum are growing between rocks. The important thing is to build the wall with stones slanted downward so that plant roots can grow naturally down toward the deeper earth in back.

Fig. 7–35. Stone walls bordering this garden were a natural as local stones were plentiful. They are laid with mortar but made to look dry by scraping out the front part of the joints. Some walls are topped with flat stones for sitting.

Fig. 7–36. In a city garden, a four-and-a-half-foot picket fence, painted white, makes a light and airy backdrop for white birches, shrubs, and flower urns.

eight by twelve inches, eight by eight by sixteen, or four by eight by sixteen) also make good low retaining walls. Just remember there is an alkaline reaction from lime in these blocks, so do not put acid-loving plants too close. Cement blocks can also be used for curbing, and the hollow centers filled with plants, herbs, or strawberries.

Fig. 7–37. This fence in a scalloped pattern with round finials every eight feet is made of redwood stained soft grey. Its curves echo those of the garden paving.

Fig. 7–38. The easiest fence to install either in country or city is cedar stockade. This fencing comes in sections and various heights from three feet six inches to eight feet, ensures privacy, and can also be used as a backdrop for a fountain or other feature.

Fig. 7–39. As a background for a perennial garden and at the same time to enclose a swimming pool, this wrought-iron fence was built of panels from the balcony of the owner's previous home. It makes a most interesting fence for this small garden.

Fig. 7–40. In order to give added height to a simple wooden fence, a lattice treatment was added to a height of eighteen inches above the top. Chinese fleece vine is growing around and through the lattice work.

Fig. 7–41. This louvered fence looks well from both sides. Vertical boards, one by six, of rough-sawn cedar are nailed to two-by-three boards and capped with a two-by-four. Redwood posts, four-by-four, can be spaced eight feet on center.

GATES, ARBORS, AND COVERINGS

Have you ever walked through a garden gate and thought "How pleasant this is!"? A gate can set the tone of your whole garden so take the time to plan it well. Unfortunately, nearly everyone living in cities or suburbs today has to be more concerned with protection and security than with charm and accessibility. Nevertheless, it is still possible to have garden gates which are both charming and secure.

Naturally, the gate is part of the fence or wall but can be made of the same or contrasting material. It can be single (two-and-a-half to four-and-a-half-feet wide) or double (five feet or wider). If it is to be used when you entertain, a double gate is more comfortable and welcoming. Gates made of wood can be reinforced for security with sturdy iron bars on the inside. Wrought-iron gates of various designs with masonry piers look very

Fig. 7–42. This double gate with wooden roof is typical of the Japanese treatment. Both sections of the gate swing inward and make an attractive way into the pool garden.

Fig. 7–43. Another wooden gate treated in the Japanese manner has only a bar across the top but gives the effect of walking through and under. The gate is made of redwood stained grey, and has openings at the top to look through. A simple wooden handle pulls the latch back.

Fig. 7–44. Brick piers are used with an iron gate. Gates such as this are available from iron dealers and come in many different designs and sizes.

Fig. 7–45. A single gate with no piers, in a slightly more elaborate design than the simple wrought-iron fence.

Fig. 7–46. The far end of a city garden was transformed into a wisteria-covered arbor made of wood with concrete columns at the outer corners. A small fountain, statue, and pool are set against the ten-foot high rear wall which dates from Revolutionary times. In winter it is particularly lovely.

Designed by owner

Fig. 7–47.   This trumpet vine (Mt. Mme. Galen) shows what one vine trained over a trellis will do for a modern country cottage. A small terrace outside the dining room is sheltered by this summer blooming vine, much loved by humming birds.

Designed by CLARA COFFEY, L. A.

graceful and are strong. Covered gates are usually double, and are particularly appropriate for a Japanese garden. The design of the gate should be considered from both inside and outside, including the direction of opening. Since gates can be heavy and are supported on only one side they should be cross braced and should have strong, durable hinges.

In small city yards there may be a chance to use a gate if you and your neighbor like to share access. These gates not only serve as a way for children to get back and forth but also can become a very decorative addition to your garden area.

Fig. 7–48.   The center section of this awning is extendable to make a protected area outside the dining room for eating. The awning is manually operated but could be worked by an electrical mechanism from a switch under the overhang.

An arbor can be a very useful and attractive feature in your garden. It can shelter a small sitting area or garden path and at the same time provide a structure for training roses, grapes, wisteria, or other vines. Style and construction materials may vary widely, from cedar saplings to aluminum or wrought iron. Materials and the openings must be chosen carefully to let in the desired amount of sun or to produce a particular shade pattern.

A metal or wood trellis attached to a blank wall enlarges garden and planting space when covered with vines or hanging containers. An overhead trellis can provide shade and a roofed-in feeling.

A solid covering for a sitting area adjacent to the house sometimes becomes a necessity if there is an excessive amount of soot or fallout. Present-day awnings are extremely easy to use when the frame is set into the house as they can be rolled up or down by electricity. Other coverings available include plain or corrugated fiberglass, transparent or in a variety of colors.

Split bamboo is an inexpensive way of covering a small area, and, like straw matting, it can be fastened to a light wood or metal frame. These have to be renewed fairly often, but they are pleasant to look at and easy to put up yourself.

GARDEN STORAGE AND TOOL SHEDS

A city gardener will need some place to hang the few tools that are needed. If there is a solid wall, one inexpensive solution would be to build a closet against it eighteen inches deep, of painted or weatherproofed wood with concrete or stone floor, large enough to hold a rake, spade, trowels, and garden hose. In another city yard, a low brick and wood structure with double doors was built for storage of outdoor cooking equipment as well as tools.

Prefabricated potting sheds and small buildings are available from many manufacturers and need only four

Fig. 7–49. This storage corner was built in as part of the design of the garden in order to provide an outdoor gas barbecue with working utensils below. It is a good serving counter also for the dining table at the right.

Designed by
JAMES S. KENNEDY, L. A.

Fig. 7–50. A built-in outdoor cabinet is ideal for storing cushions and other small movables. Stained the same color as the benches on each side, it makes an interesting table-top corner arrangement.

corner posts as foundation. They are very easy to assemble and give plenty of space to pot and putter and store the equipment needed on a country property. With a tiny terrace in front and flowers in a window box, the little building can become a feature. Or if you prefer, painted green and tucked away among the shrubbery, it will disappear into the landscape.

Some prefabs are large enough for a work bench and firewood storage, as well as tools and pots. Be sure that the door is wide enough for a wheelbarrow and any small motor equipment you may have. It is wise to have water in this area as well as electricity.

Another idea for the suburban do-it-yourselfer is to build a lean-to on the garage with space for compost and work bench.

PLAY AREAS FOR CHILDREN

Play space for children is one of the prime reasons many families seek houses with backyards rather than apartments in cities and suburbs.

Many contemporary ideas make it easier to build your own small playground. Remember that unless your family is very large this play area will be used only for a few years: one day soon it will be part of your garden design, perhaps an outdoor room for some other special project uses. On one suburban property, for instance, the play area eventually became a vegetable garden. As the children grew, they each were given plots and enjoyed this area as much as the sandboxes and swings of their early childhood.

Most youngsters can climb a low fence by age two or soon after, so keep this in mind. Temporary fencing may be sufficient and, as the children grow, can be replaced with more decorative garden enclosures.

Play equipment is a challenge to your own ingenuity. Ready-made pieces are widely available and can be assembled to suit particular terrain, trees, and spaces. But you can also do it yourself and make climbing fixtures out of the simplest materials, such as sturdy timbers with rounded edges or concrete slabs.

Figs. 7–51 and 7–52.   Wooden timbers in two formations have enough variety to keep children interested. Heavy timbers are balanced to stand of their own weight on level ground, weatherproofed and smoothed so that kids don't get hurt by splinters.

Designed by CLARA COFFEY, L. A.

Fig. 7–53.   This brick-faced wall has small set-in platforms of concrete or wood for climbing and play. Later these could be used to set out pots of all sizes and shapes with bonzai or any specimen plants.

Designed by CLARA COFFEY, L. A.

And when the children are older, you may want space for basketball practice or a badminton court. Even in my tiny city yard there was room for a tetherball post which fitted into a larger concrete anchored pipe. My children spent many happy hours at this simple ball game which only took up a space fifteen feet in diameter. Another wonderful exercise as well as exciting amusement for the small fry is the trampoline which will go into an eight-by-twelve-foot corner.

LIGHTING   And lastly, let's light the garden. Whether in city or country, a few properly placed lights that can be switched on from inside the house make a garden continue to enchant through long summer evenings and dusky winter afternoons. A snowy garden lit at night is sheer magic.

Outdoor lighting will give pleasure to all who look out on the garden from whatever vantage point, and will create a feeling of spaciousness even in a tiny area. Garden illumination should always be done in a subtle, never obvious manner and it takes considerable thought and careful planning. For the new home-owner, it should be incorporated into the original design so that the fixtures can later be put where desired, with house connections and the proper switches located near the garden doors. The circuits should connect to the main fuse

Fig. 7–54.

panel, usually coming in through the basement wall, with all outdoor wiring of the direct-burial cable type.

For an old house, installation of outdoor lighting will mean putting in a new or enlarged switch panel connected to underground circuit wiring, and drilling cable holes in basement walls.

The outdoor outlets must be waterproof, as low to the ground as permissible, and can easily be concealed by planting. Fixtures must always be shielded to prevent glare in your eyes or those of your neighbors. They can be the up-lighting type, which shine on tree branches from below; down-lighting, which picks out a clump of flowers or low shrubs; spread-lighting from a suspended overhead fixture casting a soft glow on all planting below; or back-lighting of walls or fences to silhouette trees and plants. Low wattage bulbs, twenty-five to forty watts, are sufficient, and allow you to have many small light sources rather than a few blatant ones.

Decide first on the permanent functional lighting of any doors or steps. Later, especially with spear-base fixtures, lights can be moved to create or change an effect, or to illuminate a newly added feature such as a piece of sculpture.

In addition to such features softly illuminated, I like to see a tree like a birch at night whose bark has an especially lovely texture in summer and winter. It will look magical in the spring with its new foliage, cool in the summer, and cheerful in the fall when leaves are yellow. An up-light can also be hooked into the trunk of the common city ailanthus—"the tree that grows in Brooklyn"—or to dramatize the blooms and feathery fronds of a silk tree.

8 water, features, furnishings, and wildlife

WATER   Whether standing, dripping, or splashing, water in a small area brings a delightful sound and coolness. The location of a water feature is a basic element of the overall garden plan, so important, in fact, that the rest of the garden is often planned around it. Water can be the main or central feature; used at the far end of a garden as the terminal motif, as a bird bath or wall fountain; or in a naturalistic pool with or without a little brook.

Fig. 8–1.

Almost anything can be used to hold water: a ready-made plastic or fiberglass basin (Fig. 8–1); a mason's mortar pan (Fig. 8–2); a concrete container created to your design with copings of flagstone or brick (Fig. 8–3); a lead or stone statue adapted for a fountain (Fig. 8–4); a pool lined with clay, tiles, or mosaic (Fig. 8–5); or an old kitchen sink (Fig. 8–6).

Fig. 8–2.

Secondly, you will need a pump if water is to spout

Concrete and Rocks made to fit site

Fig. 8–3.

Lead or Stone Statue

Fig. 8–4.

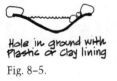

Hole in ground with Plastic or clay lining

Fig. 8–5.

old sink, tub, trough

Fig. 8–6.

or flow in and out of this feature. This means an electrical outlet nearby and usually involves a recirculating line from the pump to the fountain or waterfall.

Most pump dealers will give specifications for amount of water moved and heights of spray reached by each model on the market. Fountain-heads come in many different styles, simple or multiple outlets in plain shapes or ornamental designs. The pump should be below the water level but easily accessible since it will need frequent cleaning, particularly in the city. The electric connections must be above water level.

The third requirement is a drain. It can be a simple plug you pull, or a more elaborate system.

Two additional elements may be provided, but are not essential. One is an overflow arrangement that will keep the water at a certain level. Another is a water source close to the pool or fountain, but this is not absolutely necessary as you can fill by garden hose.

For more elaborate and expensive fountains or little streams more space is needed, but one of these plans (see Figs. 8–11 and 8–12) shows a miniature brook just twenty-two feet long which could be easily adjusted to most small garden plans.

If you want to keep fish in a pool, it should be at least eighteen inches deep so that the water will stay at a fairly even temperature summer and winter. The easiest way to kill goldfish is to have them in a hot pool.

In freezing climates lay steel or wire-mesh reinforced concrete under the pool to a depth of three feet. A little help from a mason at the outset can prevent leaks and later troubles. If a pool is to hold waterlilies, it should be at least two-and-a-half-feet deep, but for purely decorative pools just a few inches will suffice.

If algae forms in your pool there are several algaecides that will control it. If you do not have fish try copper sulphate—a few spoonfuls of the crystals in a cloth bag should clean it easily.

A few aquatic plants may add interest, but select just one or two as they are apt to take over a small pool.

Fig. 8-7. An old iron kitchen sink was painted a bright blue and sunk into the corner of a terrace. With a little frog under the bushes at left to spout water and the smallest of recirculating pumps, it makes a pleasant and very inexpensive feature in a small city yard.

You will also need to have pots for the soil and they take up space. I recommend water hyacinth, floating heart, water snowflakes, or arrowhead. If you want a waterlily, try one of the hardy small flower varieties. There are several nurseries that deal only with water plants (see Appendix B) and it is wise to consult them when you are making your choices.

Fig. 8–8. A triangular pool in the corner of a city yard shows what lush growth can develop from just a few aquatic plants.

Several shrubs lend themselves particularly to planting around water features: pussy willow, winterberry, inkberry and summersweet. Hardy flowers to grow nearby might include violets, bloodroot, iris, swamp mallows, or marsh marigolds. The little plant, creeping Jenny, is good for fast-growing ground cover along a brook.

Figs. 8–9 and 8–10. This brook is only fifteen feet long but looks as though it gushes naturally through the planting into the little pool.

A submersible pump rests on the bottom of a hidden compartment. Water is filtered as it reenters the pump to be piped to the top of the brook. A valve on this pipe controls the amount of water coming down the waterfall. The electric cable is hidden and passes through an opening in the flagstone to the outlet.

Designed by JAMES S. KENNEDY

Fig. 8-11. This circular pool with a frog spouting on the coping brings the sound of water to a small brick terrace.

Fig. 8-12. If your plan calls for a wall fountain consider a stone, brass, copper, or terra-cotta masque which you can purchase at a garden shop. Attach this to the wall and allow the water to drip into a shallow basin and then into a pool below. You will need a supply line for the water, a recirculating pump, and an overflow connection to the drainage system. Here this type of water feature has been placed in a circular niche at the end of a garden. The vine climbing over the top of the wall is *Clematis montana rubens*.

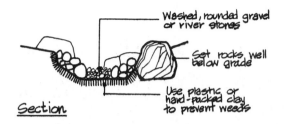

Washed, rounded gravel
or river stones

Set rocks, well
below grade

Use plastic or
hard-packed clay
to prevent weeds

Section

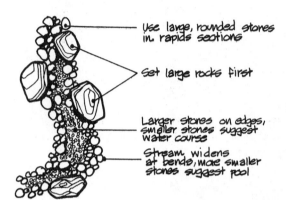

Use large, rounded stones
in rapids sections

Set large rocks first

Larger stones on edges,
smaller stones suggest
water course

Stream widens
at bends, more smaller
stones suggest pool

Plan

Figs. 8–13 and 8–14. Designed as a garden away from the house, this dry stream is located at the edge of a woodland. It could be adapted to many other sites. Stream drops only one foot in its twenty-foot length.

FEATURES   As the final phases of a garden plan develop, it will seem more and more important and enjoyable to create a special point of interest somewhere in your garden. In fact, the spot for such a feature could well be one of the earliest elements in the plan. This focal point can be as bare and functional as a wooden bench, as elaborate or

FEATURE   PLACEMENT

Central Motif

Fig. 8–15.

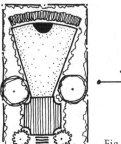

Terminal Feature

Fig. 8–16.

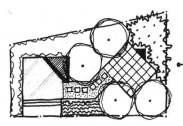

Asymmetrical Arrangement

Fig. 8–17.

Fig. 8–18.   At the edge of this narrow flower border adjacent to the terrace, a stone statue of St. Francis stands humbly looking down among the tulips and peonies. Rosa rugosa is growing on the bank behind the wall and makes a colorful background.

starkly simple as a sculpture, as sentimental as a piece of wood carved by your children for a birthday present.

Having decided on this spot in the plans, the feature must be kept in scale with the garden area. A lantern, a masque, a figurine, or even a piece of driftwood may need an architectural base and these can be purchased at many garden centers or made of cinder blocks,

Fig. 8–19. A narrow area outside a library door made a good setting for this small lead owl. White impatiens are planted in front with begonias and other house plants arranged attractively behind it.

Fig. 8–20. A large terrace overlooking one of Long Island's inlets was paved with flagstone but some special point of interest was needed in the large expanse. Three stones were removed, topsoil inserted, and a piece of driftwood arranged with painted decoys and low geraniums.

Fig. 8–21.   In the corner of a brick pier this bronze figure of a bird in flight lends sculptural interest to the garden wall.

Fig. 8–22.   A Japanese lantern placed beneath an old Japanese maple gives a mystical feeling to this small stone area which is also an easy one to maintain.

stones, or brick. Plant material may be needed as a back-drop and to draw attention to this spot. Hollies are especially good for this purpose with their shiny leaves, as are evergreens such as yews.

In a pattern garden made on a circle within a square, the pool, sundial, or other feature stands traditionally in the center (Fig. 8–15). The beds on each side can be outlined with box and filled with flowers, bedding plants like begonias, or just ivy, and the whole garden enclosed by a hedge.

In some gardens a feature may be placed at the very back of the site (Fig. 8–16). This would be a good spot for sculpture, giving perspective, or for a raised and jetting fountain. Backed by a high evergreen hedge, or a creeper-covered wall, the effect can be dramatic.

An asymmetrical arrangement with two pools may bring the sound and sight of water to a small space in an interesting way. In Fig. 8–17 we see the lower pool visible from the house in a corner with the smaller pool at a distance connected by a little path.

FURNISHINGS   Another of the finishing touches for a garden which is to be lived in is the choice of furniture. Even though the sitting space in small gardens is limited, that doesn't mean it can't be flexible and adapted to different uses and times of day. Where you eat and drink, for example, some sort of movable umbrella or permanent cover can be part of the furnishing.

New materials have eliminated many of the old problems of garden furniture upkeep. With vinyl coatings and polyesters, sun, rain, and cold no longer rust, ruin, and discolor, so furniture can remain in your year-round garden view. But wood and wrought iron still have their attractions of texture, color, and design. All-weather finishes are essential if these pieces are to be left outdoors, though many people still prefer to take them in or cover them during northern winters.

Old millstones used as tables and set on columns or

travertine marble, mosaic, glass, and decorative tiles used in tables are elements with color and texture interest which can be mixed with ready-made and synthetic chairs, benches, and loungers to good effect. I am often asked about a round table versus a rectangular outdoor dining table. No question—a round table is infinitely more useful and flexible. Remember that a standard table three feet six inches in diameter needs space double that diameter for chairs to fit comfortably around it. A chaise five feet long needs at least two additional feet of moving space. Chairs do not need to be large and cumbersome in order to be strong and comfortable. Much well-designed furniture today is light and stackable and tables collapsible for easier storage. For decks and paved gardens, casters on furniture increase comfortable use and flexibility. Even a large marble-topped bar can be equipped with skateboard wheels.

WILDLIFE   Many city dwellers become confirmed bird watchers. There is something very exciting in having wildlife in your yard. You must feed the birds if you want to keep them. The great variety of feeders, from a small tray on a post outside the kitchen window to the more elaborate feeding stands, can add much to your enjoyment of bird watching. (Audubon Workshop puts out a Bird Lover's Catalog and Handbook, illustrating types of feeders.) It is especially important to provide water, warmed in winter, for the birds in a northern garden. This is easily done by having an electrical outlet for a birdbath heater, which is an immersion-type water heater. The thermostat inside this heating element maintains the temperature at fifty degrees Fahrenheit so that the birds can have water when everything is frozen.

There are three essentials to encourage birds to visit your garden—food, water, and shelter. Food comes first. Place the feeder above the ground on a tree or post, sheltered from winter winds and in some winter sunlight if possible, and easily visible from a window. Remember to fill the feeder regularly. Varieties of birdseed are easily available even at supermarkets. Another food birds like in winter is suet, which can be put in wire cages and hung from branches.

Once you have begun to feed the birds and watch them, you will find that they come happily and bring lots of friends and relations. Birds do eat plant seeds and cause other garden damage, but I think the joy and music they bring far outweigh the nuisance.

These plants will help attract birds to your garden.

Trees

birch	holly
cedar	maple
dogwood	mulberry
hawthorn	pine
hemlock	shad

Shrubs

burning bush	russian olive
holly	viburnum
juniper	yews

Ground covers

bearberry	creeping rose
blueberry	cotoneaster

Vines

bittersweet	grape
honeysuckle	pyracantha

Other visitors and residents besides birds are helpful and should be part of the garden scene—snakes, toads, frogs, and turtles. I know of one city garden which boasts the largest turtle for miles around. It was picked up in a country pond and brought home by a small boy

**PLANTING
TO ATTRACT BIRDS**

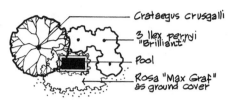

Fig. 8–23. Hawthorn and hollies are selected for their bright red berries which last through the winter and are enjoyed by the birds.

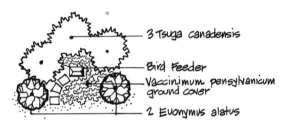

Fig. 8–24. Hemlocks will give the tree cover and background for bird feeder. Blueberry and burning bush were selected for berries.

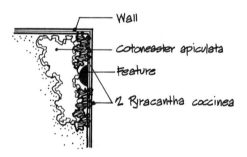

Fig. 8–25. Firethorn upright and stiff with large clusters of orange berries and cranberry cotoneaster—a good evergreen with glossy foliage and bright red berries like cranberries.

who is now twenty-five years old. Myrtle, an Eastern box turtle, loves to come out for a bit of meat when anyone appears in the garden during the warm months. Frogs and toads will live on the land but need water to breed in. The croaking of the male frogs in the spring is a wonderful part of country night music.

A word about squirrels—a controversial subject

Fig. 8–26.

Fig. 8–27.

since some people love them and others consider them pests: if you start feeding them in your garden, particularly a city garden, it can become a haven for many squirrel families. Even if you don't feed them they will come in and eat your bulbs and destroy your flowers and potted plants. Many people find them such fun to watch that they don't mind. And how can you keep squirrels out anyway?

9 my favorite plants

In the preceding chapters you have seen how to make a general plan and to consider your construction details. You are now ready to make the planting plan. With tracing paper laid over your general plan, outline in green the areas to be planted. Give some idea of the heights of plants you will need—low, medium, and tall. Make a circle for each plant. This circle should represent the size the plant will be when fully grown. This prevents overcrowding—one of the mistakes most frequently made. Plants, like children, grow very quickly and too close planting limits normal growth. Another point to consider is the plants' hardiness. In Appendix A the hardiness zones are indicated for different parts of the country and plants that are suitable for each. You can also learn the hardiness of plants by checking with your local Agricultural Experiment Station.

I have seen common dogwood growing in northern

Fig. 9–1. Flowering dogwood on the north side of the house and a clump of birch.

New York on the north side of a house where it is relatively unprotected from the strong winds, but it is protected from the more damaging, even scorching late winter sun. This site might be called a microclimate, and you may find that on your own property there are some areas like this.

As you consider the plants for your garden, study the form, eventual size, texture, and color of each plant you propose to use. Only in this way can you really know how they will fit into your garden.

Form or shape is important—it sets the scene for the picture you have in mind. Do you want to hide something in the background? Use tall, narrow trees or shrubs. Do you want trees to frame a view or give shade to a terrace? Perhaps you need a weeping tree to hang over your pool. The form of shrubs is even more noticeable, such as the forsythia which spreads wide or the low junipers some of which make little low cushions while others spread in many directions.

In regard to the size, you will probably purchase

fairly small plants particularly for the city home, as everything has to be brought through the house. But you need to note how large each one of these trees and shrubs will grow so that you do not overcrowd and buy too many plants.

Texture is something I consider very early in designing a planting plan. Some trees, like the oaks, have a coarse texture while the weeping willow has a soft pendulous effect. The hollies have a shiny sparkling green quality while the rhododendrons give a duller and coarser texture. Junipers give a feathery look while yews have a dense, heavy appearance.

Color, both in foliage and flower, must be noted. A plan that has color interest throughout the year is definitely right for a city garden and this can be carried out with proper selection of evergreens and deciduous specimens. Remember plants will not look the same in every season—in winter you will have one picture with evergreens dominant. In spring shrubs will be in bloom and in autumn leaves will be a blaze of color.

Even in my small city yard the fall season brings forth the yellow colors on the deciduous azaleas and birches, the brilliant red of the Chinese dogwood, and lastly the amber color of the magnolia.

For the person unaccustomed to selecting plants, particularly one knowing very little about them, this can be a bewildering time. If you have done your plan carefully and purchase only those plants you have listed, you can be sure your garden will mature properly.

It is necessary to check your soil to be sure that it has been fertilized and prepared for growing the particular kind of plants you want to use. It is far better to plant a five-dollar shrub in a hole that you have spent ten dollars preparing than to buy a more expensive plant and drop it in without any preparation.

In selecting shrubs, remember to use more than one of each kind—a clump of three or five is appropriate in order to avoid a spotty effect. If you know plants there are many that you will want to include but in any garden it is important to use restraint. The following lists may

help you in your decision, but do visit a nursery or botanical garden to observe the ones you select. If you can't
resist buying more plants than can fit into a well-land-
scaped garden plan, don't spoil your plan but make a
separate little section, even in a corner of your city yard.

And now consider your budget. If you want immediate effects you will have to buy larger, more costly
plants. If you can wait, perhaps five years, for your plants
to complete your design, you can begin with very small,
less expensive plants and enjoy watching them develop.
Too often people try for an immediate effect by overcrowding. In a few years, unless some plants are removed, the whole effect is ruined. Proper spacing is important at the start as plants need room to grow.

With plan completed, to facilitate ordering, itemize
the plants you want under these headings: Quantity,

Fig. 9–2. Beneath a tree where it is difficult to grow grass fill the
ground to a height of three to four inches with brick, tanbark, pine
needles, or gravel and border it with brick or railroad ties in order to
keep the surface in place. This will make a cool sitting area.

Fig. 9–3. The shape of trees is particularly noticeable when silhouetted against snow. Here in a city yard the flowering crab apples make a lovely pattern.

Botanical Name, Common Name, Size, Remarks. On your list group trees, then shrubs, vines, ground covers, and lastly, the herbaceous material which includes flowers. You can then send this list to the nurseries for estimates, or use the catalog of a nearby nursery to estimate for yourself. Add charges for delivery and planting; these may run as high as fifty percent of the plant costs. Perhaps you will prefer to visit a garden center yourself and pick up the plants on your list since many of them are now sold in carry-home containers.

Following are lists of my preferred plants in the different categories.

TREES **Street Trees**

*PIN OAK. *Quercus palustris*—fast growing, good shape.

* Plant material that will stand city conditions.

*LINDEN. *Tilia cordata*—upright with fragrant flowers.

*GINKGO. *Ginkgo biloba*—excellent for narrow space, interesting leaves; the fruits of female plants have an unpleasant odor, so get male plants.

*BRADFORD PEAR. *Pyrus calleryana Bradford*—white flowers, lovely fall color.

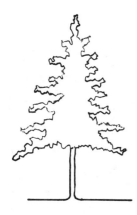

Fig. 9-4. Pin Oak.

Shade Trees

*JAPANESE PAGODA. *Sophora japonica*—spreading, summer blooming, interesting bark, lacy texture.

RED MAPLE. *Acer rubrum*—fast growing, brilliant autumn foliage.

*HONEY LOCUST. *Gleditsia triacanthos*—fine texture, filtered shade, many varieties.

Flowering Trees

*DOGWOOD. *Cornus florida* and *kousa*—native flowering and Chinese flowers, good foliage and nice fruit.

*HAWTHORN. *Crataegus phaenopyrum* and *crusgalli*—Washington and Cockspur the best; white flowers, glossy leaves, clusters of bright red fruit.

*MAGNOLIA. *Saucer magnolia, Magnolia soulangeana*, and *Star magnolia, Magnolia stellata*—saucer for large scale planting, lovely bark and beautiful flowers; star magnolia smaller scale with many early flowers.

*CRAB APPLE. *Malus floribunda* and *sargenti*—good in city and country, lovely flowers, good fruit, fast growing, many varieties.

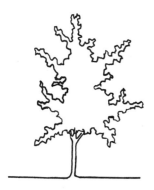

Fig. 9-5. Gingko.

Specimens

*BIRCHES. *Betula papyrifera*—selected for bark, color and shape; multiple stems.

*STYRAX. *Styrax japonica*—flowers in summer, good structure.

Fig. 9-6. Japanese Pagoda.

* Plant material that will stand city conditions.

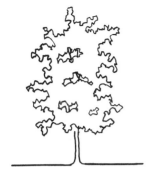

Fig. 9–7.   Honey Locust.

Fig. 9–8.   Red Maple.

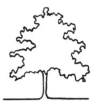

Fig. 9–9.   Flowering Dogwood.

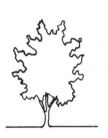

Fig. 9–10.   Chinese Dogwood.

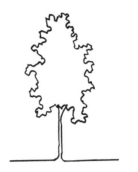

Fig. 9–11.   Bradford Pear.

Fig. 9–12.   Sargents Crab.

Fig. 9–13.   Crab Apple.

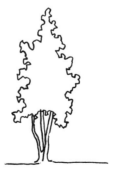

Fig. 9–14.   Birch.

Fig. 9–15.   Styrax.

Fig. 9–16. Japanese Maple.

Fig. 9–17. Hawthorn.

JAPANESE MAPLE. *Acer palmatum* and *palmatum dissectum*—both good small trees.

*CHERRIES. *Prunus yedoensis*—gets big, nice shape. *Prunus serrulata Kwanzan*—stiff shape but easily available and lovely flowers.

Weeping Trees

WEEPING CHERRY. *Prunus subhirtella pendula*—lovely flowers, interesting form.

WEEPING BIRCH. *Betula pendula*—good accent plant for special sites.

*RED JADE CRAB. *Malus Red Jade*—small with long pendulous branches, white flowers, red fruit.

Evergreen Trees

PINES. White pine, *Pinus strobus;* Japanese black pine, *Pinus thunbergi*—both fast growing.

HEMLOCKS. *Tsuga canadensis*—rich green foliage.

SPRUCE. *Picea omorika*—graceful arching branches, fast growing.

SHRUBS   **Low-Growing**

Deciduous Shrubs   *GLOSSY ABELIA. *Abelia grandiflora*—summer blooming pink flowers, lovely bronze foliage.

*COTONEASTER. Many varieties from low creeping ones to tall upright; shiny leaves, red berries.

ST. JOHNSWORT. *Hypericum Hidcote*—summer blooming, big yellow flowers.

BUSH CINQUEFOIL. *Potentilla fruticosa*—in variety, blooms from June to November in shades of yellow.

Medium

*REGAL'S PRIVET. *Ligustrum obtusifolium regelianum*—common, easily grown, berries attract pheasants.

* Plant material that will stand city conditions.

*FORSYTHIA.   Arnold dwarf—a good low-growing, spreading variety.

*EUONYMUS ALATUS AND ALATUS COMPACTA.   Interesting corky branches, bright red autumn foliage.

High

LILACS.   *Syringa vulgaris* and hybrids—both hybrid and common excellent spring-blooming plants.

*RUSSIAN OLIVE.   *Elaeagnus angustifolia*—silvery gray foliage with orange fruit; good near the sea.

*VIBURNUM.   These are the three I suggest: *Carlesii* (fragrant), *Dilatatum* (linden), and *Tomentosum* (doublefile).

Specimen

TAMARIX.   *Tamarix chinensis*—blue-green foliage, pink flowers, interesting all year.

WINTERBERRY.   *Ilex verticillata*—a deciduous holly with bright red berries, good in moist places.

*ENKIANTHUS.   *Enkianthus campanulatus*—upright shrub with clusters of bell-shaped flowers, brilliant autumn color.

Evergreen Shrubs

DWARF PINE.   *Pinus strobus nana*—excellent specimen plant.

HEMLOCK.   Sargent weeping hemlock, *Tsuga canadensis pendula*—very graceful, slow growing in sun or shade.

JUNIPER.   Excellent for sunny positions; great variety of shapes and color. My favorites are *Juniperus horizontalis*, Bar Harbor, *Wiltonii*, *Sargentii*, and *procumbens nana*.

*LEUCOTHOE.   *Leucothoe fontanesiana*—arching plant with excellent winter color, will stand shady conditions; good in spring when flowers bloom.

* Plant material that will stand city conditions.

Fig. 9–18.   Vitex, tamarix, and summersweet behind a low box hedge.

LAUREL.   *Kalmia latifolia*—wonderful native plant to use; will grow fairly fast, flowers in June.

* YEW.   Excellent for year-round effect; bear no flowers but useful for hedges, specimens and fillers.
Taxus baccata repandens. T. cuspidata—many varieties including *nana* and *densa. T. media*—many varieties. *Hicksii* and *Hatfieldii* are good uprights for hedges.

* ANDROMEDA.   *Pieris japonica*—lovely tall plant with white panicles in the early spring; *floribunda* is low-growing and arching.

   * Plant material that will stand city conditions.

Fig. 9–19. Beneath a dogwood, Japanese and mountain andromeda with drooping leucothoe and myrtle as ground cover.

MY FAVORITE PLANTS FOR AZALEA GARDENS

Azaleas will flower from April till July if you select the right varieties. There are numerous ones to choose from and they do not mind being planted while blooming. They come in many different colors, evergreen and deciduous. They need at least five hours of sunshine a day, acid soil, and watering weekly in dry seasons from May to August while they are setting their flower buds. Fertilize with Hollytone after blooming.

Deciduous Native Varieties

SWAMP. *Arborescens*—white flowers in May, lovely autumn foliage.

ROYAL. *Schlippenbachii*—large pink flowers in May.

PINKSHELL. *Vaseyi*—pink flowers in April and May.

SWAMP. *Viscosa*—white flowers in June.

Plants to Bloom from April through June

Glen Dale

Aphrodite—rose pink   *Gaiety*—rose pink
Cygnet—white   *Greeting*—single orange

Gable

Louise Gable—salmon   *Springtime*—violet red
Rose Greeley—white   *Stewartstonian*—red

Kurume

Apple Blossom—white   *Peach Blow*—salmon

Exbury

Gibraltar—orange red   *White Swan*—clear white,
                               fast grower

Vuyk

Palestrina—large white

Fig. 9-20. Azalea Delaware Valley in the foreground with Palestrina behind the bird bath.

Additional Favorites

Balsaminaeflora—peach, low growing

Daviesi—white blotched yellow

Delaware Valley White—white, best of the evergreens

Gumpo—pink and white, very low growing

Kiusianum alba—white, low

Narcissiflora—yellow double flowers

Polaris—white, good in shade

RHODODENDRONS FOR THE SMALL PLACE

Small-leaved

The small-leaved varieties do extremely well in the city. They need an acid soil and some shade and protection from the winter winds.

RHODODENDRON KEISKEI.   Lemon yellow, dwarf.

* RHODODENDRON P.J.M.   Rose purple, low, rich bronze winter foliage.

* RHODODENDRON RAMAPO.   Blue violet, gray green foliage.

RHODODENDRON DORA AMATEIS.   White blossoms in May.

* RHODODENDRON WINDBEAM.   Soft pink, good foliage.

Large-leaved

CATAWBIENSE.   Rosy lavender, good for mass planting.

MAXIMUM.   Tall, white to pink, glossy foliage, best in the shade.

Varieties

AMERICA—bright red.

BLUE PETER—lavender blue with dark blotch.

* BOULE DE NEIGE—white, low growing, and compact.

GOLDSWORTH YELLOW—creamy yellow flowers.

Fig. 9–21. In the city hybrid rhododendrons flourish along this path.

JOHN WISTER—light pink, compact.
MRS. C. S. SARGENT—deep pink, glossy foliage.
NOVA ZEMBLA—red, good habit.
* ROSEUM ELEGANS—pink to lilac, upright growth.
SCINTILLATION—pink, broad habit.
WHITE GEM—white, low growing.

HOLLY GARDENS

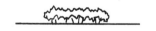

Fig. 9–22. Helleri

Hollies are wonderful plants to use for year-round effect in many different places as they range in size from a foot to tree size and have glossy foliage and fruit. They require acid soil, well drained with organic material, and male and female plants are necessary for fruit. Mulch with oak leaves. All hollies will stand city conditions.

Fig. 9–23. Convexa

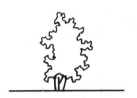

Fig. 9–24. Crenata

Fig. 9–25. Pedunculosa

Fig. 9–26. Aquifolium Opaca

JAPANESE HOLLY. *Ilex crenata*—many varieties, small leaf, spineless, black berries.

> *Convexa*—spreading boxlike foliage.
>
> *Helleri*—low growing, compact.
>
> *Rugosa*—very low spreading.
>
> *Stokes and Green Island*—rounded habit.
>
> *Blue Boy and Blue Girl*—fine upright foliage.

CHINESE HOLLY. *Ilex cornuta Burfordii*—glossy leaves, needs a sheltered spot.

ENGLISH HOLLY. *Ilex aquifolium*—glossy deep green foliage, red berries; *Camelliaefolia* is one of the best. May need winter protection.

INKBERRY. *Ilex glabra*—native plant, black berries, rich glossy foliage turns bronze in winter.

LONGSTALK HOLLY. *Ilex pedunculosa*—upright like birch, fast growing, smooth leaves, hanging clusters of red berries.

AMERICAN HOLLY. *Ilex opaca*—native holly; best varieties are Hedgeholly, Old Heavyberry, Nellie Stevens, and Canary with yellow berries.

PLANTS FOR SHADY CONDITIONS In selecting plants for your shady garden bear in mind that conditions vary greatly from low swampy areas to high dry hillsides, from dense to light shade, and from acid soil to alkaline. Some existing trees may have to be removed so that you can make an interesting layout using some plants from the following list.

Fig. 9–27. Old Japanese holly pruned in "cloud formation" to give an interesting shape.

Trees to Grow in the Shade

* Dogwood, *Cornus florida*
Hemlock, *Tsuga canadensis*
* Holly, *Ilex* species, American and English

* Plant material that will stand city conditions.

Hornbeam, *Carpinus carolinianum*
Redbud, *Cercis canadensis*
Shadblow, *Amelanchier* species

Shrubs to Plant under Trees

* Andromeda, *Pieris japonica* and *floribunda*
Chokeberry, *Aronia arbutifolia*
* Leucothoe, *Leucothoe fontanesiana*
Mountain laurel, *Kalmia latifolia*
Rhododendron, native species and hybrids
Summersweet, *Clethra alnifolia*
* Viburnum, especially species *dentatum, lentago, prunifolium*

Ground Covers under Trees and Shrubs

Bugleweed, *Ajuga* species
* English ivy, *Hedera* species
* Myrtle, *Vinca minor*
Pachysandra, *P. terminalis*

Herbaceous Flowering Plants

Astilbe, in variety
Bleeding heart, *Dicentra eximia*
* Bluebells, *Mertensia virginica*
Day lily, *Hemerocallis thunbergi* hybrids
Epimedium, several species
Jacob's ladder, *Polemonium caeruleum*
* Patience plant, *Impatiens holstii*
* Plantain lily, *Hostas* species
Primulas of many kinds
Windflower, *Anemone hupehensis*

* Plant material that will stand city conditions.

Fig. 9–28. A path created through existing woodland and outcropping rocks was designed to have winter interest with pines, laurel, and rhododenron, and planted for spring color with early deciduous azaleas and drifts of narcissus and primula.

Designed by
CLARA COFFEY L. A.

WILD FLOWERS AND FERNS

For many hours of pleasure, try starting a collection of wild flowers. You can find and collect a great many of these plants growing in their natural habitat. Be sure you dig only the ones you will use and if you buy from a nursery get the plants that will do well in your area. Tuck these into corners and along paths and enjoy them without a great deal of work—they seem to thank you for bringing them into your garden.

These are the ones that I have had success with:

Wild Flowers

Bloodroot, *Sanguinaria canadensis*
Dog's-tooth-violet, *Erythronium americanum*
Galax, *Galax aphylla*
Golden-rod, *Solidago varieties*
Jack-in-the-pulpit, *Arisaema triphyllum*
Queen Anne's lace, *Daucus carota*
Sweet woodruff, *Asperula odorata*

Trillium, *Trillium grandiflorum*
Violets varieties
Wild ginger, *Asarum canadense*

Ferns

Christmas fern, *Polystichum acrostichoides*
Cinnamon fern, *Osmunda cinnamomea*
Hay-scented fern, *Dennstaedtia punctilobula*
New York fern, *Dryopteris noveboracensis*
Royal fern, *Osmunda regalis*
Toothed or common wood fern, *Dryopteris spinulosa*

GROUND COVERS Ground covers are valuable to cover surface below shrubs, to discourage weeds, to cover banks, and to grow where grass is impossible. They need six inches of well-prepared topsoil.

* MYRTLE. *Vinca minor*—creeping evergreen plant with blue flowers; excellent in the shade.

BUGLE. *Ajuga reptans*—several colors blooming in June and July; makes excellent mat.

CREEPING COTONEASTER. *Cotoneaster dammeri*—low-growing shrub, bright red berries.

EPIMEDIUM IN VARIETY. Six to ten inches high, in various colors with heart-shaped leaves.

SARGENT JUNIPER. *Juniperus chinensis sargentii*—low-spreading shrub, good winter color, needs sun.

*PACHISTIMA CANBYII. Low evergreen, six inches to one foot, small dark green leaves.

LEADWORT. *Plumbago larpentae*—summer blooming, perennial, lovely blue flowers from July to frost.

FOAM FLOWER. *Tiarella cordifolia*—low growing, increasing by runners.

* IVY. *Hedera helix*—both English and Baltic are excellent.

* Plant material that will stand city conditions.

Fig. 9–29. Junipers covering the planted area along a path give a feathery texture.

LILY OF THE VALLEY.   *Convallaria majalis*—lovely fragrant flowers.

VINES   Vines are one of the easiest and most helpful plants to use—easy because they require little attention and helpful because they contribute so much in a short time. Be sure to select the right one: if it is for a fence use roses (on the posts not in between); on a downspout try fleece vine; on a trellis use clematis. If you have an arbor, either wisteria or grapes will cover it in a few years. If you want to cover a north wall or chimney, use climbing hydrangea. But in each case consider the color and texture of the one you select.

Supports and wall-type nails will be necessary in some cases. Prepare soil deeply so strong roots can develop. Apply fertilizer in the spring and mulch in the fall. Water is very essential during the growing season. Early training is necessary to get vines started in right direction. Thereafter some pruning may be necessary to keep them properly trained.

Fig. 9–30. The large white flowers of this hybrid clematis bloom for a long period.

CLEMATIS. Needs limey soil, shade at roots, top part in sun.

> *Montana rubens*—deep pink flowers in June.
> *Paniculata*—sweet autumn, fragrant white flowers in September.
> *Jackmanii*—blooms on new wood, prune, rich purple.
> *Lanuginosa candida*—large white flowers.

* CLIMBING HYDRANGEA. *Hydrangea petiolaris*—clinging vine with fragrant white flowers in June, likes shade.

> * Plant material that will stand city conditions.

Fig. 9–31. This wooden fence with its trained ivy is interesting throughout the year and especially in the winter when snow covers the ground and outlines the pattern of the English ivy.

*FLEECE VINE.   *Polygonum auberti*—greenish white flowers in August, very fast growing.

*WISTERIA.   White and purple blooming, does well in city but a rampant grower and must be controlled.

FLOWER GARDENS   When flower gardens are mentioned one usually thinks of a separate garden room planted in a formal or informal way but there are many other places you can use flowers—along a path, in front of evergreens, beside a brook, and of course on your terrace.

Sunlight is essential for flowers, although a few perennials such as iris and day lilies will stand some shade. Annuals such as marigolds, petunias, and geraniums will grow well provided they have sun and moisture. Spring bulbs, however, will give the greatest satisfaction especially to the city gardener.

In working out a plan for a flower garden, draw it at one quarter inch to one foot scale. Make a list of the flowers you want to use and indicate whether they are low-edging plants, accents like peonies, or tall background plants. Then select the fillers. These will constitute the largest number of flowers and here is where to work at getting a succession of bloom. In order to do this well a border should be at least four feet wide, or as wide as seven feet if it can be reached from both sides.

Fig. 9–32. A five-foot bed of coral colored geraniums below a railroad-tie wall with an edging of begonias makes an attractive feature for a summer garden.

MY FAVORITE FLOWERS

When you consider the composition of your garden, aim for an arrangement of pleasing forms, textures, and colors in foliage and bloom, placed to create a harmonious grouping.

Perennials

These are among the most easily-grown perennials and will give continuous bloom in a small garden over many months.

Edging Plants
Candytuft, *Iberis* varieties—May
Coral Bells, *Heuchera sanguinea*—June, July
Accent Plants
Peonies—June
Balloon Flowers, *Platycodon*—June
Filler Plants
Iris, *Iris* varieties—June
Astilbe, *Astilbe* varieties—July
Columbine, *Aquilegia*—May
Poppies, *Papaver* varieties—June

Phlox, *Phlox* varieties—July, August
Speedwell, *Veronica longifolia subsessilis*—August
Chrysanthemums, in varieties—September
Tall Plants
Delphinium hybrids—August
Asters, *Aster Harrington's pink*—September
Helen's flower, *Helenium Riverton Gem*—August,
September

Daylilies   Hemerocallis—daylilies are very hardy, long-blooming,
require minimum care; and can be massed in beds for
stunning summer color.
Little Cherub—May
Atlas, Caballero—June
Hyperion, Tinker bells—July
Boutonniere, Mrs. Wyman—August
Autumn Prince—September

Lilies   Lilium—lily bulbs are planted in late fall; they need a
well-drained site. Plant in groups among perennials or
even among low-growing shrubs.
Madonna, Candidum—June
Mid-century hybrids—June
Regal Lily, Regale—July

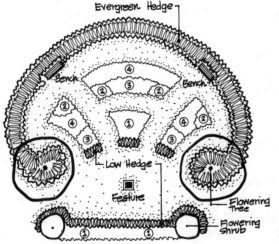

Fig. 9–33.   Suggestion for a small annual flower garden: 1. Petunias; 2. Zinnias; 3. Blue Salvia; 4. Marigolds.

> *Olympic Hybrids*—July
> *Speciosum*—August
> *Auratum*—August

Annuals   The mainstays for summer bloom; they give continuous color and are excellent for picking.

Ageratum	Marigolds
Alyssum	Petunias
Begonias	Spider plant
Blue salvia	Tobacco plant
Impatiens	Zinnia

ROSES   Roses are perhaps the most beloved and probably the most demanding of flowers and yet I couldn't do without them, for even one rose picked fresh every morning makes the whole day more beautiful. I feel that roses should be planted in groups in a stylized fashion, and their beds edged with a low evergreen hedge and backed up with a fence or taller hedge as a foil for their color. Avoid plantings of roses mixed among other shrubs or flowers both for aesthetic and horticultural reasons.

Roses need rich soil preparation, careful spacing, regular spraying and feeding. For the beginner any of the current books on roses will be helpful and should be consulted.

Here is a list of my favorites among the various kinds of roses you might wish to use.

Climbers
    Golden Showers, yellow
    New Dawn, pale pink
    Paul's Scarlet, Old-fashioned, red

Hybrid Teas
    Charlotte Armstrong, deep pink
    Chrysler Imperial, dark red
    Eclipse, yellow
    Garden Party, white
    Pascali, white
    Peace, yellow blend

**PLAN FOR A SMALL
ROSE GARDEN**

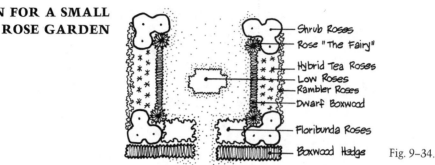

Shrub Roses
Rose "The Fairy"
Hybrid Tea Roses
Low Roses
Rambler Roses
Dwarf Boxwood
Floribunda Roses
Boxwood Hedge   Fig. 9–34.

     Tiffany, pink to salmon
     Tropicana, orange red

Floribundas
     Apricot Nectar, apricot blend
     Betty Prior, pink, continuous bloomer
     Fashion, coral pink
     Saratoga, white
     Vogue, flame

Grandifloras
     Buccaneer, yellow
     Queen Elizabeth, pink

Miscellaneous Roses
     Frau Karl Druschki, white
     Harison's Yellow, deep yellow
     Rugosa, pink and white
     The Fairy, pink

BULBS Two of the most exciting times in the garden come in October when you plant your bulbs, and then in the spring when you have the joy of seeing them come to life in all their glorious colors. Make your selection from one of the good bulb catalogs and *do* order them no later than August so you will be sure to get the varieties you want. Allow plenty of time for poring over a catalog as there are many, many colors and shapes from which you will have to make your choice. It need not be an expensive selection: twenty-five dollars will buy enough to make a nice showing in a corner of your garden.

Fig. 9–35. Three dozen tulips planted against an old boulder give a splash of color just outside the library window. The deep purple of the double Uncle Tom and the pink favorite Clara Butt make a nice contrast against the weathered stone. Boxwood and junipers frame this small planting.

Consider the bulbs in relation to your house and terrace so that you can see them as they are blooming in the spring. Tuck them into planted areas in front of your evergreens, outside of the library windows in your perennial garden, or among the rocks on a hillside. They can also be naturalized in a woodland planting, or planted in containers to bring out on the terrace.

You must prepare the bulb beds properly by digging down nine inches and you must be sure there is good drainage. You can add bone-meal fertilizer—five pounds to 100 square feet. Plant your bulbs as soon as they arrive, water them in, and then wait until spring. After the bulbs have finished blooming, I suggest that you leave them in the ground and fertilize with bone meal again as this helps to strengthen the flower buds for the following year.

Certain narcissi are best for naturalizing in woods or along the edge of your garden. These include: February Gold, Carlton, Mrs. Krelage, Rembrandt, Cheerfulness, Actaea, and Beersheba. If you should be late in planting these bulbs it is a good idea to soak them for fifteen or twenty minutes before you plant them.

Plant in irregular groups. For example under a forsythia or birch you could use twenty-five narcissus bulbs with fifty of the small bulbs like crocus or scilla.

My favorite bulbs are listed below.

Small Bulbs   Crocus species, *Chrysanthus* and *Tomasinianus*
Hyacinths, selected colors
Scilla sibirica and *Campanulata*
Snowdrops, *Galanthus elweisii*
Snowflake, *Leucojum aestivum*

Narcissi   Beersheba
Cheerfulness
Golden Harvest
Liberty Bells
Mrs. R. O. Backhouse
Thalia

Tulips   Species for Early Bloom
Clusiana
Kaufmanniana
Red Emperor

Species for May Bloom That Blend Well Together

Pink
Clara Butt
Princess Elizabeth
Rosy Wings

Shades That Blend with Pink and Yellow
Ambrosia
Dido
John Ruskin

Yellow
Moonlight
Mrs. Moon

Shades That Blend with Yellow and Lavender
Don Pedro
Louis XIV

Lavender and Purple

> Anton Mauve
> Blue Perfection
> The Bishop
> White
> Mt. Tacoma
> White City
> Zwanenburg
> Red
> Red Matador
> Scarlett O'Hara

VEGETABLE GARDENS   Growing your own vegetables is a pleasure not only for the fruit of your labors but for the inner joy of accomplishment you will feel. I know of one busy executive whose garden is not particularly beautiful to look at but produces marvelous vegetables and gives him much-needed relaxation and exercise. Never having grown even a radish before, he now has great success with everything he plants. He has learned a lot, and his family and friends benefit from his hobby.

Vegetable growing in the city is not easy, but if your yard has at least six hours of sun a day and the soil is adequate, you will probably be successful. If the soil is very poor, you can use raised planters filled with a mixture of garden loam and peat moss and still obtain excellent results. Water is easily supplied to a small area and insects can be more easily controlled. However, sunshine is the most important ingredient.

Plan your city vegetable garden in the sunniest spot of your yard. If possible, do not put it right in the middle for it is not always a thing of beauty. Place it in a corner or in front of a little greenhouse. You won't need much in the way of tools and supplies: only a spade, a rake, and fifty pounds of fertilizer (5–10–5 or five percent nitrogen, ten percent phosphorous, five percent potassium—nitrogen makes green growth; phosphorous helps plants to flower and bear fruit; potassium gives the general healthy tone).

Be sure to plan your garden on paper and don't overplant the first year. To begin a vegetable plot, dig and turn the earth well in the spring to a depth of one foot, breaking up lumps and clearing out any stones or rubble. Be sure it is well drained as vegetables will not grow in wet soil. Go out and look at the plot after a rain. If it stays muddy, you will need something to lighten the soil—sand or soil conditioner. A few days later add fertilizer and mix well with the soil before planting.

Buy small plants the first year but after some experience you may want to grow some vegetables from seed,

Fig. 9–36.   A greenhouse six by eight feet in a city yard grows all of the seeds for the small vegetable garden. By continuous replanting, food for the family is produced for six months of the year.

Fig. 9–37. A country vegetable garden with its picket fence serves as one of the garden rooms on this suburban property.

other than bean and radish seeds which are always put directly into the ground. A few tomato plants, eggplant, peppers, and string beans make a good beginning. Several kinds of lettuce will give a variety of salad combinations. Do not try to grow corn or potatoes in a small area as they take a lot of room. Squash and cucumbers also take up a great deal of space unless they are trained to grow on a fence. They need a large area to spread in order to produce enough for an average family.

If your vegetable bed is to be raised for drainage, it should be at least four feet wide and twelve inches above ground level. Retaining walls can be of railroad ties or cinder blocks. Always loosen the existing soil below before adding new topsoil as drainage is an important factor.

Figures 9–36 and 9–37 show some of the various and satisfying crops which can be produced even in small city backyards. If there is space, you might add a dozen raspberry bushes. In one garden these produced twenty pints of berries the first year, a great luxury for the city dweller.

For the suburban or country gardener, select a place that is sunny, away from trees, not too far from the house, and accessible to water. It will probably need a fence or a surrounding hedge of marigolds to keep animals away.

Choose a site where your plot can be expanded if needed, as long as the drainage is good. My favorite sites are on one side of the garage or behind it if there is room, or a real Williamsburg type of vegetable garden with picket fence, roses, and paths of tanbark or brick. The paths can be bordered with fruit trees or blueberry bushes.

If the site is very steep, it is advisable to terrace it with railroad tie walls. If it lies on a gentle slope, be sure to run the rows crosswise to the slope so the seeds won't be washed away in heavy rains. On level ground and wherever possible, plant the rows north and south so that all vegetables get the same amount of sunshine.

Now you must decide what vegetables to grow. In a small space, say ten by fifteen feet, there just isn't room for everything. Plant vegetables that you know grow well in your area and that your family likes. This probably means lettuce, beets, carrots, radishes, stringbeans, onions, and tomatoes. As you gain experience you will change the varieties and probably add other kinds. Your first success may lead you to enlarge the size of your garden, which means more work, weeding, and watering, but gives produce for freezing as well as eating fresh-picked. A good idea is to plant varieties of the same vegetable that are ready for picking at different intervals.

Follow the basic rules for garden preparation, and remember that weekly maintenance keeps your garden in a healthy condition. You will then enjoy fresh and flavorful vegetables all summer as well as saving money on your grocery bill.

HERB GARDENS   Herb gardens are another part of outdoor living which adds zest to your life and your cooking. The perfect place is a spot near the back door which is sunny, has good soil,

Fig. 9–38. If you have the space, there is nothing nicer than a real herb garden, one you can walk in to enjoy the many fragrances surrounding you.

Fig. 9–39. A built-in container on a wide deck has a planting of herbs where they can be easily reached and enjoyed throughout the summer.

and is easily accessible. The city dweller might plan for just a few herbs that can be pinched for seasoning. If space is very limited, one idea is to set sections of round or square hollow clay chimney pipe into the ground and plant different herbs in each, making a colorful pattern, or knock the bottoms out of terra-cotta flower pots. You can make a small square raised bed with railroad ties set on the narrow side. Mints, especially, need an area that can be controlled. Chives, parsley, dill, sage, sweet basil, lavender, and tarragon are among the most useful and easily grown herbs.

Many herbs—such as sweet basil, summer savory, and marjoram—can be grown from seed. The perennials lavender, sage, and rosemary are best purchased as seedling plants. Once you have planted a few herbs you will always want to grow them. Besides being excellent for

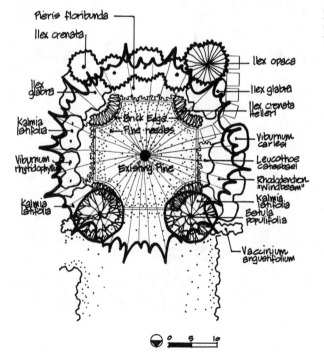

Fig. 9–40. Beneath the shade of a pine tree a brick-edged terrace is surrounded by plants that like acid soil conditions.

cooking, salads, and drinks, they make delightful little gifts when dried.

PLANTING SKETCHES   With just a few plants it is possible to create an interesting landscape effect. These little planting sketches show what you can do in various sections of your garden in the city or country.

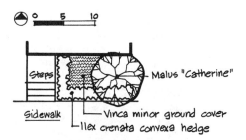

Fig. 9–41.   The front yard can be treated simply with a boxwood holly hedge, *Ilex crenata*, ground cover of myrtle, *Vinca minor*, and a flowering crab apple, *Malus Catherine*, which has white blossoms followed by yellow fruit.

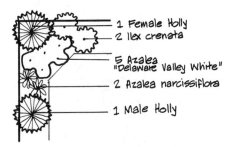

Fig. 9–42.   A corner planting for year-round interest might include a female holly, of American, English, or Chinese variety, with the male plant not too far away. Two Japanese hollies, *Ilex crenata*, give a shiny green effect throughout the year. Color can be added with azaleas. Here I have suggested white and yellow.

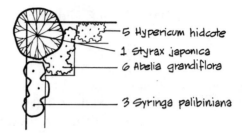

Fig. 9–43. For bloom in the summertime
there is nothing more attractive than an
upright Styrax japonica with its white blossoms and unusual bark. Abelia and Hypericum also bloom throughout the summer.
Lilacs, *Syringa palibiniana*, bloom in June
with pale lavender blossoms.

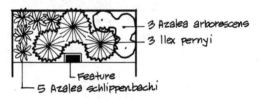

Fig. 9–44. Surrounding a feature Chinese holly
(*Ilex pernyi*), provides bright red berries and
shiny dark foliage throughout the winter. Additional planting includes azaleas, Royal (*Schlip-
penbachi*), and Sweet (Arborescens) selected for
their white and pink spring blossoms and their
coppery fall leaf color.

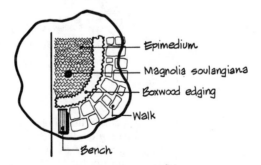

Fig. 9–45. Beneath a magnolia tree where a
bench has been placed there is a boxwood edging with a ground cover of epimedium which
has heart-shaped leaves and white, yellow, or
pink blossoms.

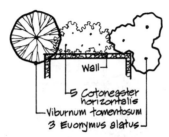

Fig. 9–46. Behind a low wall three burning bush *Euonymus alatus*, are planted for autumn color. The single large double-file viburnum (*Viburnum Tomentosum*) was selected for its horizontal habit and white flower clusters. The ground cover is rock cotoneaster.

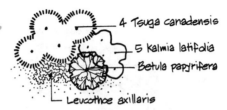

Fig. 9–47. A country garden might need to be closed in with evergreen planting such as several hemlocks (*Tsuga canadensis*), laurel (*Kalmia latifolia*), and a white birch (*Betula papyrifera*). Low leucothoe gives color in the fall and winter.

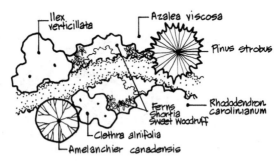

Fig. 9–48. Along a woodsy walk a shadbush or serviceberry (*Amelanchier Canadensis*) blooms in early spring with feathery white flowers. Next to bloom are the Carolina rhododendrons and fragrant swamp azalea. (*Azalea viscosa*.) Ferns, shortia, and sweet woodruff edge the path. In winter the pine (*Pinus Strobus*) and the red buttons of deciduous winterberry (*Ilex verticillata*) remain to give color.

197

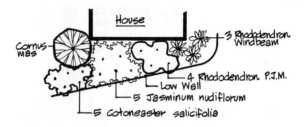

Fig. 9–49. Against a stone house yellow winter jasmine (*Jasminum nudiflorum*) blooms in late winter, followed by the yellow blooming dogwood (*Cornus mas*), the P.J.M. Hybrid rhododendron, and the rhododendron windbeam. Ground cover is willowleaf cotoneaster (*Salicifolia*).

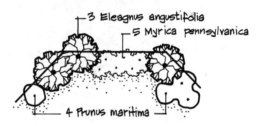

Fig. 9–50. A planting near the seashore might include Russian olive (*Eleagnus angustifolia*), bayberry (*Myrica pennsylvanica*), and beach plum (*Prunus maritima*).

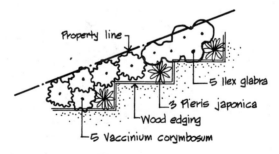

Fig. 9–51. A sloping property line can be made most interesting by stepping back the planting bed. In a shady area Japanese andromeda (*Pieris japonica*), inkberry (*Ilex glabra*), and a high bush blueberry (*Vaccinium corymbosum*), are planted together to make a pleasant arrangement.

Fig. 9–52. Three old forsythia and privet shrubs were pruned into natural arches to form a natural gazebo. A large boulder was cleared of honeysuckle, the area leveled, and an old stone bench moved in, making a wonderful place for children to play and grown ups to pause and read or look at the view.

10 planting fundamentals

After designing the garden and doing all the construction work, you are now ready to order the plants and do the planting. What you hope is that each tree, shrub, and ground cover will grow well for you and that your garden will flourish. But the plants will grow only if the soil is adequate—loose, mellow, friable loam. You can add humus, peat moss, and fertilizer and dig in to a depth of eighteen inches to provide the necessary nutrition. Remember, you must have good drainage as water standing at the roots of plants will quickly kill them.

Soils in the eastern part of the United States are predominantly sand or clay. Before you start, it is wise to have an analysis made so that you will know what your soil contains. Clay soil is slow to warm up; it does hold moisture but it will need sand, humus, compost, or leaf mold to provide good growing conditions. Sandy soil warms up sooner but is apt to dry out; it may be planted earlier and is easy to work but will need humus, peat moss, or leaf mold. As a rule, to improve existing soil conditions I recommend adding to every 150 square feet: one bale of peat moss, fifteen pounds of lime (unless acid-loving plants are to be planted), and four to five pounds of 5–10–5 fertilizer.

The question often arises as to whether one should fertilize at planting time or wait until later. In general, I feel that it is wise to do it at planting time to be sure the fertilizer is well incorporated into the topsoil. Do not work your soil when it is wet because it cakes.

I recommend that you buy plants from nurseries or garden centers, rather than from supermarkets. They should be freshly dug and their roots should not be exposed to the air. When you plant them, work the soil in so that there are no air pockets around the roots. Thereafter it is necessary to water thoroughly once a week throughout the first year depending upon the weather. If it has been a particularly windy week, for example, plants will need more water than when it is still.

Mulches are helpful to both city and country gardens as they keep weeds down and hold moisture. Be sure to spread the mulch at least two inches deep in order to make it effective. Mulches you can buy include:

- *Pine bark* comes in coarse, medium and fine. One bag will cover twenty square feet.
- *Salt hay*, one bale covers 1000 square feet.
- *Buckwheat hulls*, one bale covers eighty square feet.
- *Wood chips* are often available from garden centers.

After the ground has frozen, it is wise to put down another layer of mulch to prevent plants from heaving as the earth thaws and freezes again.

A yearly program of feeding, especially for city plants, is essential. If you have planted rhododendrons, hollies, and azaleas, I recommend using Hollytone and cottonseed meal in equal proportion in late March or early April. Quantities depend on size of the plants as directed on the package.

Spring is also the time to consider pruning. Trees and shrubs are pruned for three reasons: for profit, as when fruit trees are cut back to make them bear more; for the aesthetic appearance of shrubs and flowering trees; for the health of the plant, which means removing dead or diseased branches. Pruning is a complex matter as each plant has different growing habits. It is wise to learn to do this yourself rather than leave it to someone else. There are many specialized books on pruning and courses given by botanic gardens and garden clubs. Knowing how pruning should be done is really the only way to avoid other people's costly and ugly mistakes.

In general prune in:

- *Winter*—Grape vines, fruit trees.
- *April*—Roses, hydrangeas, buddleia, and tamarix.
- *May and June*—Flowering shrubs such as forsythia, lilacs, and mock oranges (after they have bloomed).
- *June*—Azaleas and privet.
- *July*—Wisteria, hemlocks, and yews.
- *December*—Hollies, for Christmas decorations.

In the city, plants need hosing or washing once a week to remove dust and soot. In regard to diseases and insects, keep a careful watch to see whether anything has infested your garden.

For winter protection of evergreens in a windy spot use one of the wilt-proof sprays in late November and again in early March. This prevents undue transpiration of moisture and allows the plant to keep a rich green foliage all winter.

Compost building can prove a valuable and inexpensive method of improving your soil. The portable compost containers which have come on the market fairly recently offer several advantages to the gardener with limited space. They are of plastic, rigid on the sides with an air-bubble plastic cushion top which allows proper aeration but keeps off direct sunlight. Their size is about that of an oil drum, but their light green color makes them unobtrusive, far less unsightly than a garbage can. Leaves and all organic refuse can be used, with soil as in any compost heap.

CARING FOR A SMALL GARDEN

January and February

Protect evergreens in snow storms by shaking branches to prevent breakage from weight of snow.

Watch for egg masses of tent caterpillars on wild cherry and apple trees and remove infested branches.

This is a good time to thin out trees and brush.

Prune fruit trees and grape vines.

Remove bag worms on evergreens and deciduous trees and shrubs.

Cut cedar galls out of red cedars and junipers.

March

Cold frames should be prepared with a good seeding soil. Keep them closed for about a week to warm up the soil before planting.

Repair work on the lawn should be done and regular feeding begun. Rake and aerate the ground and feed with twenty-five pounds of organic fertilizer to 1000 square feet.

Spray lilacs and other deciduous shrubs that have scale with a dormant spray, such as Scale-O, Scalecide, or Sunoco Spray Oil. The dilution is usually one part of oil to fifteen parts of water, with a teaspoon of nicotine sulfate. Apply on a bright sunny day when temperature is about forty-five degrees F. Bittersweet, euonymus, and pachysandra may also need this.

Feed trees and shrubs that are well established with a complete fertilizer.

Order dahlias and other summer blooming bulbs.

April

In perennial gardens remove some of the winter mulch and clean up. Burn all trash. Spray peonies with a good fungicide against botrytis blight.

Spray* evergreens for scale and gall aphids with a

* The new licensing laws on sprays and spraying require all operators to be licensed. The home owner should check on all details of the law before doing any spraying.

dilution of one part miscible oil to twenty-five parts of water.

Prune roses, removing diseased canes; plant new roses and feed existing bed with 5–10–5 or a special rose food at the rate of a trowel full per plant. Work well into soil.

Shrubs and trees can be planted early in the month, evergreens towards the end of the month.

Sow annuals in cold frames—tomatoes and other vegetables can be started there early in the month.

In perennial gardens, fork the remaining mulch into the soil and check for plants that have died. Reset any plants that have heaved.

Spray delphiniums for mites with an approved miticide, and also stir in wood ashes around the roots. Make cuttings of chrysanthemums. Remember that anemones, plumbago, and platycodon are slow to appear, so do not dig them up. Transplant pansies to their permanent position. Feed the garden with bone meal, wood ashes, and compost, the amount depending upon soil condition. Start a weekly program of cultivation one to two inches deep to kill weeds and conserve moisture.

May This is an important time to have the trees sprayed for chewing insects. Watch box for leaf miners and spray them and birch trees that have been attacked by the birch-leaf miner with a systemic insecticide.

Spray hollies for leaf miner with a systemic. Use an approved fungicide for leaf spots or blight of mountain laurel, Virginia creeper, or Boston ivy or hawthorn.

Azaleas, rhododendrons, and other broad-leafed evergreens should be fed now with a special acid fertilizer.

Watch yews for taxus weevil infestation (this can be noticed when growth does not start or if needles turn brown.) Use a systemic spray on ground.

Prune early-flowering shrubs such as forsythia by cutting out the older wood.

Spray or dust roses with nonpoisonous Sevin and Benlate (for black spots) and apply mulch by end of month. Spray ramblers for mildew with Mildex.

Start seeds in outdoor garden—vegetables of all kinds and flowers such as sweet alyssum, marigolds tall and dwarf, zinnias, nicotiana, and cosmos.

In the perennial garden fill bare spots with new plants. Spray phlox for spider mites and for mildew with Mildex. Spray iris with Sevin and Benlate to check borer and control leaf spot. Spray lilies for botrytis. Feed peonies, iris, and other perennials coming into bloom and continue weekly cultivation.

June   Water all newly planted trees and shrubs. Spray rhododendron, azaleas, pieris, and mountain laurel for lace bugs and have elms and willows sprayed for leaf beetles.

Treat lawns for chinch bugs with nonpoisonous Sevin.

Cut hedges now. Watch thrips which attack privet hedges and spray with nicotine sulphur and soap.

This is the month for roses—so enjoy them, but continue feeding and spraying them. Remove dead roses by cutting close to a five-leaflet leaf—never pinch off flowers and leave a long stem.

In perennial gardens plant annuals and chrysanthemums. Also plant geraniums, begonias, and summer blooming bulbs. Keep chrysanthemums pinched back and mulch to check leaf nematodes. Spray lilies with Benlate. Divide iris after blooming. Continue weekly cultivation.

July   Water is essential during hot dry spells. Once a week use soil soaker which gets water down to roots—never sprinkle overhead.

Midsummer brings problems of red spiders on evergreens—strong sprays of water help to prevent this.

If scale still continues on euonymus and lilacs spray them with an approved scalecide. Birches may need another spraying with a systemic insecticide.

Prune climbing roses. Remove all old wood at the ground line as they will bloom next year on new shoots now being produced. Large-flowered climbers bloom on old wood, so remove only old flowers and enough canes to keep the plant within bounds. Continue weekly spraying of roses.

In perennial gardens spray for mildew again and transplant overcrowded iris and any that have rot. Water phlox frequently and do not let it go to seed. Cut back perennials that have bloomed. Pinch back chrysanthemums, except early varieties, and spray if necessary for aphids and mildew with Rotenone and Benlate.

August   If you have boxwood now is the time to clean out all old leaves that hold moisture to help check the canker that is apt to attack now. Burn all leaves. Spray with an approved fungicide.

Continue watering.

Watch for lace bugs on azaleas and spray with Malathion.

Lawns need watching. If chinch bugs appear, spray again with Sevin. Crab grass can be controlled now with specialized weed killers but keep them away from shrubs, trees, and any broad-leaved plants.

Roses may be fed for the last time. Continue spraying.

In perennial gardens, watch for dodder which is a tiny, turning, parasitic vine that wraps itself around your plants. All of vine which has orange tendrils must be removed. Stake chrysanthemums and start feeding them. Water phlox frequently and remove blossoms that have finished blooming. Continue weekly cultivation.

Order spring-blooming bulbs now to insure getting desired varieties.

September   Lawns should be fed again and if reseeding is necessary, now is the time to do it. Ease up a little with the lawn mower. If water is needed use it lavishly at longer intervals rather than often and sparingly.

Check dogwoods, lilacs, and rhododendrons for borers. Crown canker is the most serious disease, attacking trees after transplanting or injury; avoid wounding trees with lawn mowers, etc.

This is a hard time for specimens set out last spring;

keep them mulched well and watered. Light shade over small plants will help check evaporation.

Shear deciduous hedges for the last time if necessary.

Continue spraying and watering roses—when cool nights appear you can expect plenty of buds.

Bring in plants to be carried over for next year and all house plants.

Plant evergreens, narcissus, and peonies (eyes two inches below surface.) Fertilize established plants with bone meal and muriate of potash.

Make new borders; start transplanting and dividing perennials.

October   Finish planting perennial borders.

Plant deciduous trees and shrubs.

Dig up and store gladioli and dahlias.

Plant bulbs, especially the small ones.

Make root cuttings, hardwood cuttings, and evergreen cuttings (to be grown indoors.)

Prune out dead and older wood from shrubs.

November   Finish planting hardy bulbs, tulips, etc.

Continue to plant deciduous trees and shrubs. Be sure they are securely staked; low-growing ones do not need much staking.

Plant roses except in the most northern areas. Hill up as planting is done. See that all climbers are cut back and firmly tied.

Rake up leaves and put on compost pile or in separate pile for leaf mold.

Be sure newly planted perennials are labeled; also bulbs in borders.

Lift and store in cold frame chrysanthemums to be used for cuttings in spring.

Hill up and mulch between roses.

December   Cover perennial and rose beds after first hard frost with salt hay or evergreen branches.

Spread mulch of partly decayed leaves or manure around trees and shrubs.

index